The Black
Adolescent Parent

The Black Adolescent Parent

Stanley F. Battle
Editor

The Haworth Press
New York • London

The Black Adolescent Parent has also been published as *Child & Youth Services*, Volume 9, Number 1 1987.

The Haworth Press, Inc., 10 Alice Street, Binghamton, NY 13904–1580
EUROSPAN/Haworth, 3 Henrietta Street, London WC2E 8LU England

Library of Congress Cataloging-in-Publication Data

The Black adolescent parent.

Includes bibliographics.
1. Adolescent parents—United States. 2. Adolescent mothers—United States.
3. Afro-American youth. 4. Afro-American families. 5. Unmarried mothers—
United States. I. Battle, Stanley F. [DNLM: 1. Adolescent Psychology. 2. Blacks.
3. Illegitimacy. 4. Parents. 5. Pregnancy in Adolescence. WS 462 B6273]
HQ759.64.B42   1987   306.8'74'088055   87-332
ISBN 0-86656-554-X

The Black Adolescent Parent

Child & Youth Services
Volume 9, Number 1

CONTENTS

Foreword

There has probably never been a time for Black people during their odyssey in America when Black scholars were more urgently needed to define the circumstances, needs, and imperatives of Black family life and the development of Black children. Blacks are once again being assaulted by "Moynihanism" — the perceptions of White scholars and media about the status of Black families and their children. White America's latest analyses come wrapped in concern for the escalating problem of teenage pregnancy and births by Black girls. As usual White scholars and helping professionals would like to control the diagnosis and prescription for Black adolescent parents and their offspring.

The editors and contributors to *The Black Adolescent Parent* provide constructive countervailing insights and advice designed to shift control of analysis and prescription into Black hands. It is a book long overdue and will go a long way toward righting the wrongs spawned by White scholars and "helpers" in the past.

One important aspect of this Black perspective is overcoming the usual neglect of the needs of Black male adolescents. The fostering of their "invisibility" has resulted in the denigration of Black males and has led to "helpers" pursuing failed strategies which dealt with only one dimension of the human interactional equation for Black adolescents. Through this process of neglect, Black male adolescent parents have been pushed into a posture of irresponsibility because their behaviors were considered to be irrelevant. Consequently, a focus in this book on Black male adolescent responsibility and functioning is indeed refreshing.

The Black sociocultural reality of the extended family and the reaching out of Black adults to youth in trouble have been misconstrued by some observers to be a character flaw in Blacks, thereby promoting unacceptable social behavior such as teenage pregnancy and births. It is crucial Black adults understand their attitudes and the messages they transmit to Black children concerning sexuality, pregnancy, and parenting. The time has come for Black adults to be clearer about what they think and want for their children and family life. This volume appropriately addresses this requirement.

ix

   The collective condition for Black family life will not be altered for the better without changing the environmental context for Black parents and their children. This enhancement requires that Black people and their leaders shape every social institution which impacts on the growth and social development of Black children. Nothing short of a collective agenda designed by Black institutions and leadership, and carried out on a collaborative basis will yield results. Black leadership is now charged with the responsibility to create a new contextual reality.

   Black adolescent parents and their children are always in jeopardy of becoming locked into America's underclass. The lack of decent job opportunities and social supports for this population heightens the probability of chronic economic dependency through public welfare or involvement in the underground economy. However, adolescent parenthood does not have to result in falling into a bottomless pit of dependency and incompetence. Fortunately, the authors of *The Black Adolescent Parent* have illuminated constructive paths for taking Black control and responsibility for the Black condition. It is my hope that Black adolescent parents and their helpers embrace the understanding and guidance offered in this important volume. If they do, the future will be far brighter for Black family life in America.

Hubert Jones
Boston University

Preface

How truly refreshing it is to see a book devoted entirely to the plight of Black adolescent parents. Far too often, one has to search reams of literature to find information pertaining to this population. The status of Black adolescent parents clearly deserves to be discussed and analyzed. They represent our next generation, and they are raising the children of the future. These factors have great consequences for Black people in America as Black adolescent parents carry the torch we pass to them. We look to them to keep up the relentless struggle against the negative effects of racism and oppression.

However, it is of great concern how Black youth may prepare themselves and their children effectively for the fight against racism and oppression in America. A wide assortment of issues cause Black adolescent parents to run the risk of being a lost generation. A higher incidence of unemployment combined with lower levels of educational attainment often leads to poverty for them. For this population, the prospects for escaping poverty appear bleak if effective intervention from federal, state and local governments, as well as private sources, is not forthcoming.

An additional untapped resource for adolescent parents lies in the Black community. We have the ability and means to instill hope in those who are facing social and economic despair. Black organizations — such as the National Association for the Advancement of Colored People, the National Urban League, the National Association of Black Social Workers, fraternal and civic organizations, and churches — can provide a variety of services to assist these young people. We can volunteer our time and energy to be role models and expose them to the knowledge we have gained over the years. We can challenge the negative mandate this country has charted for our youth.

Leading the struggles, we must develop opportunities so Black adolescent parents may have the means to raise healthy and viable families. The positive and essential ramification of this is the creation of a generation of motivated and self-assured Black youth who will guide their families to new heights. Additionally, these young people will be prepared to work more effectively to overcome social, economic, and political injustice.

After all, we want for Black children what all parents want for their children: the opportunity to raise prospering families who can share in the American dream. This book provides us with a means to understand better the plight of Black adolescent parents in our society; it will help us to refine our approaches, programs, policies, and attitudes so we can more effectively assist our Black youth. Read it carefully and refer to it often, for there is a generation seeking change and opportunity who are depending upon it.

Peter R. Correia III, MSW
University of Oklahoma

Acknowledgements

This book is the result of encouragement from many people. I particularly wish to acknowledge Dean Hubert Jones of the School of Social Work, Boston University, and Peter A. Correia III, Associate Director of the National Resource Center for Youth Services, University of Oklahoma.

I am very grateful for the technical assistance and friendship of Maria Iantosca, MSW. She made a very difficult process manageable. I also wish to acknowledge Shelley Chamberlin for her organizational efforts during the early stages of this project.

Finally with love and gratitude, I thank my wife, Judith Lynn Rozie Battle, and our daughter, Ashley Lynn Battle, for their love and support.

Stanley F. Battle

Introduction

Research on adolescent pregnancy has proliferated in the last decade. We now have a substantial body of empirically-based findings in this area. Unfortunately, few substantive findings are available on the Black adolescent parent, yet the magnitude of this problem has reached epidemic proportion. In 1978, it was estimated that nearly twelve million teenage men and women were sexually active and on the average began sexual activity around sixteen years. Today it is the exception to find a young person who has not had premarital intercourse by the age of nineteen.

This special issue was conceptualized to examine the complicated problems faced by Black adolescent parents. All contributors to this text realize it is quite naive to assume that one book on Black adolescent parents will answer all the questions, but it is a serious attempt to explore the nature of this problem in depth. How does a Black adolescent girl experience pregnancy and parenting? How does the Black adolescent father feel about his responsibility toward the mother of his child? Why are the birth rates for Black adolescents higher than for other teenagers in America? How does the Black community respond to this problem? We must begin to address and answer these types of questions if we desire to assist this population.

Taborn begins this issue by examining issues uniquely relevant to Black adolescent parents. He overviews engagement in sexual activity, birth control, reactions to pregnancy, abortion, and adoption. Special emphasis is devoted to the Black experience.

A comprehensive literature review by Franklin on adolescent pregnancy follows. Causes and consequences of pregnancy are identified, as Franklin balances qualitative and quantitative material.

Through a series of clinical interviews Boxill describes in realistic terms how Black adolescent mothers view themselves. Many of these mothers are scared, and they have limited parenting skills. Also many are on AFDC, with a history of limited educational achievement. Boxill focuses on four themes relating to Black adolescent mothers: perceived failures of their own parents; the lack of satisfactory intimate relationships with peers and others; the experience of being simultaneously too young and too old; and the challenge of becoming a good mother.

Three chapters focus on programs designed to meet the needs of adolescent parents. Barnett interviewed twenty Black adolescent mothers who were active in a multiservice childcare program in a large alternative inner-city school. These mothers had an opportunity to identify problem areas related to their needs and services. Findings centered on qualitative aspects of services, for instance, how these mothers evaluated the level of respect extended to them, the treatment and value of the information provided. Evans provides an examination of Black adolescents who were mothers or at risk for pregnancy. His sample includes forty-five Black adolescent females between 16-17 years of age. Since the sample size was small, findings suggest that attitudinal risk factors are important in understanding causality and prevention of adolescent pregnancy.

Dunston and Hall next examine Black adolescent parenting from a familial context. They provide a valuable review of programs that serve adolescent mothers, as well as describing a pilot program that extended its services to include the families of Black adolescent mothers. Examining this pilot program allows the authors to highlight strategies for providing services within a familial framework.

Black adolescent fathers are not left out of this special issue. Hendricks and Solomon present a discussion on how to reach Black adolescent fathers through nontraditional techniques. This population has been ignored by the practice community for many years, usually as a result of ignorance and misunderstanding. The authors gathered their data from a cross-sectional study of 133 first-time, unmarried Black adolescent fathers who reside in Tulsa, Oklahoma, Chicago, Columbus, Ohio, and Washington DC.

This special text is concluded by Battle and Battle who examine privacy rights and how the Black family is affected when their teens have children. Adolescent parents and the grandparents are faced with many problems centering around moral and legal responsibilities. The Black family is a unique institution, and frequently, the methods utilized by the courts and by families to address problems do not coincide. The authors also examine the Black parents' perspective as well as family planning concerns.

The contributors to this text are all Black and have a unique interest in the quality of this publication. They are aware that the problem of Black adolescent pregnancy has overwhelming implications for the stability and future of the Black family. Nearly 60 percent of all Black children are born out of wedlock. Black adolescent females between 15 and 19 are the most fertile of that age group in the industrialized world. Half of all Black adolescent females become pregnant. Almost half of all Black children are partially supported by government programs. Clearly, the Black community cannot ignore these findings. The predictions of a permanent underclass and of chronic economic dependency are outcomes that are becoming institutionalized. Discussion must take place in communities and in academic settings. It is my hope that this book will offer some direction in that regard.

Stanley F. Battle

EXCLUSIVE FOREIGN SALES REPRESENTATIVES
FOR *THE HAWORTH PRESS, INC.* JOURNALS

Separate price lists are available from the following exclusive foreign sales representatives. All new or renewal orders must be sent through these sales representatives only for the territories specified.

AUSTRALIA, NEW ZEALAND, AND THE SOUTH PACIFIC ISLANDS (including Papua New Guinea, the Fiji Islands, the Solomon Islands, and New Caledonia): D. A. Book (Aust.), Pty., Ltd., 11-13 Station Street, Mitcham, Victoria 3132, AUSTRALIA.

BRAZIL: Publicacoes Technicas Internacionais Ltd., R. Peixota Gomide 209, 01409 Sao Paulo-SP-BRAZIL.

INDIA: Allied Publishers Subscription Agency, PO Box 155, 13/14, Asaf Ali Road, New Delhi-110002 INDIA.

JAPAN: Maruzen Co., Ltd., 3-10 Nihonbashi 2-Chome, Chuo-Ku, Tokyo 103 JAPAN.

MALAYSIA, SINGAPORE, AND BRUNEI: Parry's Book Center, PO Box 10960, 50730 Kuala Lumpur, MALAYSIA.

MEXICO: DIRSA MEXICO (Distribuidora Internacional de Revistas, S.A.) Georgia No. 108, Apdo. Postal 27-374, MEXICO, 18, D.F.

PAKISTAN: PAK-BOOK CORPORATION, Aziz Chambers, 21, 21-Queen's Road, Lahore-3, PAKISTAN.

PEOPLE'S REPUBLIC OF CHINA: China National Publications Import and Export Corporation, P.O. Box 88, Beijing, PEOPLE'S REPUBLIC OF CHINA.

SOUTH AMERICA (excluding Brazil), including Uruguay, Argentina, Chile, Paraguay, Venezuela, Colombia, Ecuador, The Guyanas, Bolivia, and Peru: DIRSA INTERNACIONAL, Plaza Independencia 848, Palacio Salvio-Escritorio 315, Montevideo, URUGUAY.

TAIWAN: Good Faith Worldwide International Co., Ltd., 9th Floor, No. 118, Sec. 2, Chung Hsiao E. Road, Taipei, TAIWAN 100 R.O.C.

The Black Adolescent Mother: Selected, Unique Issues

John M. Taborn

ABSTRACT. This chapter examines recent findings concerning attitudinal and behavioral variables that impact upon Black adolescent females who are sexually active and who may become mothers. Key questions are raised and decisions evaluated that relate to the probability of a teenager's becoming pregnant. Key decisions prior *and* subsequent to becoming pregnant regarding the Black adolescent female are included: Is she able to conceive? Has she become sexually active? Does she use contraception? If pregnant, does she choose to abort or carry her child to term? Does she place her child for adoption or keep the child? Significant findings from recent research are provided at each step of this process, along with broad suggestions for adapting human service programs and treatment strategies to accommodate the unique needs of the Black adolescent female.

Unwed motherhood among adolescents in the United States has reached alarming proportions, in spite of more public information and advances in medical technology in contraception and other birth control methods. The United States has the second highest teenage birthrate among thirty developed nations (Hungary has 103 births per 1,000 adolescent girls and the U.S. has 101 births). For Black adolescents (under age 18) in the U.S., the current rate is 237 per 1,000, compared to 71 births per 1,000 for White teenagers (Taborn & Battle, 1984).

John M. Taborn, MA, PhD, is Associate Professor in the Department of Afro-American and African Studies, University of Minnesota, with associated appointments in the Psychoeducational Studies Department and the Center for Youth Development and Research. He is also in private practice. Dr. Taborn has devoted much of his career to studying the mental health of minority groups, as well as the impact of racism as it affects personal and organizational functioning in the public and private sectors. He also consults to public and private agencies and has published extensively.

1

While the proportion of childbirths among Black adolescent females exceeds that of adolescent White females, mortality of infants of Black adolescent females also exceeds that for White females: 23.1 per 1,000 for Blacks compared to 12.0 per 1,000 for Whites (Taborn & Battle, 1984). The death rate for minority children is 70 percent greater than for Whites.

The vast and crucial topic of Black adolescent parenting demands examining the adolescents themselves, their family life, their economic opportunities or struggles, and their beliefs. Human service professionals need to become aware in specific terms of the plight of Black young people, for the meaningful sexual expression of these adolescents can lead to pregnancy. The problems and joys of pregnancy are very real to these teens and their needs must be reckoned with if they are to be able to make choices that are right for them.

What do Black adolescent females think and feel about their sexuality? Their relationships that include sexual expression? What do they think about their chances of becoming pregnant? What will be the course of their life if they do become pregnant? What about their children? These questions are vital to these young women, their families, and to all of us who work with them.

The issue of unwed Black adolescent motherhood poses several dilemmas for members of the helping professions. When compared with Whites, Black adolescent mothers tend *not* to have abortions and tend *not* to place their newborns for adoption. Thus human service professionals need to develop strategies to deal with the unique issues associated with Black adolescent sexuality, strategies which by necessity have to differ somewhat from those developed for the majority group.

While similarities among adolescents of various racial and cultural groups probably far exceed the differences, the differences affect key decisions that often result in adolescent pregnancy. These important variables must be re-examined for they should influence the development of culturally-specific program or treatment models, both preventive and interventive. It is equally crucial that Black adolescent females *not* be perceived as a monolithic group, and that additional demographic variables be given some weight in program or treatment designs.

We may examine selected critical issues affecting unwed motherhood among Black adolescents by following a chronological sequence of critical events in their lives. The results of comparative studies highlight intervention issues and suggest direction for helping Black adolescent females understand themselves better.

Key areas to be addressed by professionals wishing to intervene with unwed adolescent mothers are: Have they reached the age of fecundity? Are they able to conceive? Do they engage in sexual intercourse? Do they use contraception? If they become pregnant, do they abort or carry their child to full term? If they carry to full term, do they place their child for adoption or keep their child?

AGE AT FECUNDITY

The age at which an adolescent female is able to conceive (age of fecundity) is obviously a critical factor in developing programs to reduce teenage pregnancy. However, the onset of menarche is considered to be a somewhat imperfect indicator of the beginning of a female's reproductive years. The age then at which an adolescent female is fully capable of conception is difficult to determine. Some writers (Presser, 1978) suggest adding two or three years to the age at menarche to make a better estimate of the age of full fecundity. Most data suggest that the typical age range of onset of menarche falls between nine and sixteen years, with most females experiencing menarche at age twelve (Presser, 1978).

When making comparisons across racial groups, national data have suggested that Black females tend to be younger at menarche than White females (U.S. Department of Health, Education and Welfare, 1973). This same source describes the median age at menarche as 12.8 years. However, other local and regional studies (Presser, 1978) indicate the reverse, that is, White females tend to be younger at menarche than Black females. The study by Presser (1978) conducted in New York City found that Black women reported a later age (12.7) at menarche than White women (12.3). The Presser study also revealed a strong correlation between age at menarche and date of first birth. There was a weaker yet still statistically significant relationship between these two variables for White females. More specifically, the Presser data found a high correlation for Blacks between late age of menarche and first births in the late twenties.

There appear to be few overall correlations between age at menarche and age of first birth. For Blacks, however, the age at menarche still appears to be highly correlated with age of initiation of sexual activity (Zelnik & Kantner, 1977). This finding has ramifications for sexual activity since the age of fecundity is estimated to arrive approximately two years after menarche; the birthrate for adolescents under age 14 is increasing; and the finding that ". . . menarche invariably gave rise to the dawning of and desire for the experience of sexual (coital) participation" (James et al., 1977). These one to two years between age at menarche and age of fecundity would seem critical months for more intensive sex education, gaining knowledge of contraception, and discussing appropriate sexual behaviors.

ENGAGEMENT IN SEXUAL ACTIVITY

Given the onset of menstruation, endocrine forces and pituitary growth, sexual activity increases. In addition, many psychological and social forces bombard the female as she moves into adolescence. A critical factor of special relevance to the issue of unwed adolescent pregnancy involves the female's decision whether or not to engage in sexual activity. There is an evident causal relationship between increased premarital sexual activity among adolescents and the risk of adolescent motherhood. Zelnik's and Kantner's (1977, 1980) surveys reveal that unmarried Black and White teenagers are experimenting with sex at increasingly earlier ages. Their study suggests that Black adolescents tend to initiate sexual activity approximately one year earlier than White adolescents; also premarital sex among Black females, ages 15-19, rose from 53 percent in 1971 to 65 percent in 1979. This figure may be compared to a corresponding increase for White females of 23 percent in 1971 to 42 percent in 1979. Thus while the rate of premarital sexual activity among Blacks is higher than for Whites, the rate of *increase* of such activity among Whites over the past few years almost doubles that of Blacks.

Comparing variations in sexual activity between Black and White adolescent females may provide important insights for practitioners. Two of the more significant research findings are that: (1) Sexually-active White teenagers tend to have a higher frequency of sexual activity than sexually-active Black teenagers (Zelnik & Kantner,

1980); and (2) Sexually-active adolescent White females tend to have more sexual partners than sexually-active adolescent Black females (Zelnik & Kantner, 1980; Semens & Lainers, 1968).

One study (James et al., 1977) found that among Black adolescents, the frequency of sexual interaction was relatively high: 25 percent of those between 14-16 years reported having intercourse once per week; 28 percent, twice a week; 10 percent, up to three times per week; 6 percent, once a month; and, 10 percent, twice a month. However, the same study revealed that these same subjects tended *not* to have many sexual partners. The authors report: ". . . sex partners were never on the scene together. Rather one succeeded another after an affair which usually lasted for months and as long as a year" (p. 632).

Thus when devising social service or counseling intervention strategies for Black females in heterosexual relationships, it might be prudent to go beyond the mere deliverance of information. It may be necessary to consider that for many sexually-active Black adolescent females, the relationship with a sexual partner may have deeper meaning than experimentation; more personalized, intensive counseling may be required.

Earlier sociological studies concerning the sexual values of Black families placed considerable emphasis on the mores of Blacks of lower socioeconomic status (Bernard, 1966). These accounts tended to attribute a relatively high incidence of sexual activity to Black females based partly on the impact of variables such as class, segregation, economic necessity, and supposed emasculation of Black males.

Over twenty years ago, Vincent (1961) discussed the fallacy that illegitimacy among low-income Blacks was an accepted way of life in Black culture. He points out that the proponents of this biased view confusingly view the consequence (unwed pregnancy) as the only researchable issue, while perceiving sexual attitudes and behaviors as unresearchable.

Johnson (1972) conducted a seminal study of 50 Black AFDC clients by administering a questionnaire concerning parental attitudes toward premarital sex. She found that older Black parents (over 30) significantly rejected premarital sex while those age 29 and under were more permissive. In addition, the most important variable affecting the nonpermissive attitude of Black mothers toward teenage coitus was their own marital status: Married Black parents were more conservative than unmarried Black parents.

Hence, family structure, parents' marital status, and parents' age may be strong factors mitigating against the view of monolithic Black permissiveness.

A more recent study of attitudes toward premarital sex was conducted by Roebuck and McGee (1977). Their findings also revealed that Black family structure had significant influence on the sexual permissiveness of adolescent daughters. These observations support findings by Johnson (1972) that daughters of matriarchies tended to be more permissive than daughters from patriarchal homes. At the same time, differences in socioeconomic status tended to have little impact on *expressed* sexual attitudes, although concomitant behaviors were not compared.

Butts (1981) explains the earlier onset of sexual activity among Black teenagers as being a product of a Black "sex-positive culture" wherein the arousal of sexual feelings does not produce high amounts of guilt, and where Afro-Americans are better able to accept their sexuality as part of their African cultural origins.

In a longitudinal study of Black and White teenagers, Jessor and Jessor (1975) found that when compared with virgins, nonvirgin adolescents had higher scores for deviance, parental acceptance of deviance, and peer acceptance for modeling of deviance. The had lower grade point averages in school, lower personal acceptance of parental controls, and low expectations for personal achievement. Nonvirgin girls placed a high value on affection and social criticism.

High self-esteem appeared to be associated with nonvirginity among boys but not among girls. Chilman (1977), reviewing several studies in the area, suggests that a positive attitude toward education, higher levels of educational achievement, and clear educational goals appear to make premarital coitus less likely for both Black and White adolescent females.

For those practitioners working with Black adolescent females, the variables of socioeconomic status and family structure appear to be important considerations for planning effective preventive and interventive strategies. In addition, a background in and understanding of the culture of Black Americans would be advantageous, especially to avoid possible "deviant" clinical assessments (i.e., lack of guilt implies psychopathology or what is assumed to be promiscuity really is having relationships with very few partners, etc.) and to plan further counseling with cultural atunement.

USE OF CONTRACEPTION

A female adolescent, who has reached the age of fecundity and who is sexually active, could do much to reduce the risk of unwed adolescent parenthood if she ensured that some type of contraception were used.

Washington (1982) reviews studies by Zelnik and Kantner (1980): While there has been an increased participation in sexual activity among all teenagers, there is a concomitant improvement in the use of contraceptives (53 percent for Whites and 76 percent for Blacks). Also Washington observes that the greatest increase in contraceptive use for Blacks has occurred most recently — since 1976.

Among teenagers in general, why some sexually active girls become pregnant while others do not is an important question. Furstenberg (1971) states:

> Quite clearly, one reason is that some girls are more fortunate than others. Low fecundity, irregular sexual relations and sheer chance allow a percentage of girls to reach marriage without becoming pregnant . . . it is still puzzling that so many do leave matters to chance. After all, the use of contraceptives would permit them to enjoy sexual relations while removing risk of pregnancy. (p. 193)

In his study of 337 unmarried Black teenagers, Furstenberg (1971) found that experience with birth control for these adolescents was related to how their mothers viewed sex. The mother's influence seemed to be based on the nature of the male-female relationships of their children, with contraceptives used more often by adolescent couples who maintained an ongoing relationship.

In spite of some Black mothers' interest in and support of birth control, there appears to be a gap between such support and the *effective* transmission of relevant, useful information to adolescents. Smith et al. (1982) found that while adolescents tended to be aware of where to get birth control, they demonstrated a lack of understanding of the menstrual cycle and its relationship to intercourse. In a comparative study of Black, Hispanic and White teenagers, Namerow and Jones (1982) report that among birth control users, Black and Hispanic adolescents were more likely than Whites to prefer oral contraceptives, while a greater percentage of Whites used diaphragms, condoms or foam. The literature does not address the interface of cultural differences vis-à-vis convenience factors.

Sexual perceptions are further revealed by Zelnik and Kantner (1979) who report that Black adolescents, when compared to Whites, are more likely to see themselves at risk of becoming pregnant; less likely to believe themselves protected by the "time of the month"; and more likely to have reservations about contraception. The authors concluded: "The unexpected character of the sexual encounter, and dependence on a safe time of month are the principal reasons for non-use of contraceptives" (p. 292).

Finally, Black adolescent females are heavily impacted by the attitudes and desires of their male sexual partner. Johnson (1972) notes that single Black females tended to report a high amount of disapproval of family planning (contraception) on the part of their male sexual partners.

Attitudes of 48 Black unmarried adolescent fathers were gathered by Hendricks and Fullilove (1983). Their findings suggest that absence of feelings of personal control over one's destiny (an external locus of control) is more likely to be associated with men who do not use contraceptives. These same men likely do not believe that condoms help prevent pregnancies.

Finkel and Finkel (1978) studied Black, Hispanic, and White sexually active urban males. They found that Black and Hispanic males were "ineffective contraceptors"; the most frequent reasons for their not using contraceptives were either their lack of preparation for sexual intercourse or their lack of concern if their partner became pregnant.

In another study, Hendricks and Fullilove (1983) illustrate that among Black adolescent fathers, those with less that a twelfth-grade education tended to believe that birth control is for girls only. Conflicting findings by Vadies and Hale (1977) suggest that Black urban males tended to place responsibility for contraception on the female, but the authors further suggest that this attitude may be changing to embrace increased male responsibility for contraception.

Apparently, among Black adolescent females, the factors associated with the use or nonuse of contraception are complex and unclear. While there is some evidence of increasing contraceptive use by this group, there is a great need for more information and education to be delivered at an earlier age than is the current practice. Because the Black female may have a deep emotional involvement with her sexual partner (though the reverse emotional attachment may not be there), some extended efforts to work with sexually-active Black males and couples should be considered.

REACTIONS TO PREGNANCY

Many studies (Smith et al., 1982; Namerow & Jones, 1982; de'Anda, 1983) reveal that the most adolescent females express being initially surprised and unhappy about becoming pregnant. However, they appear to be able to become reconciled with the fact of pregnancy in a relatively short time, tending to become happy about their expected parenting.

In a study of Black, Hispanic, and White adolescent mothers in their third trimester of pregnancy, Held (1981) found that while Blacks tended to have the harshest reaction to their initial awareness of pregnancy, they tended to have the highest self-esteem score by the third trimester. Accepting the fact of pregnancy creates a need for the Black adolescent female to make important decisions concerning her future. Given the opportunities available in today's society, the first decision involves the youngster's answer to the question, ". . . abort or carry the baby full term?"

ABORTION AND THE BLACK ADOLESCENT

The Guttmacher Institute (1981) reported that in 1978, 434,000 teenage pregnancies ended in abortion. Of this number, 362,000 were out of wedlock. Zelnik and Kantner (1974) observed that among unwed pregnant White adolescents, 41.5 percent terminated their pregnancies by abortion; and 48.9 percent carried their babies to term. The corresponding figures for Blacks were quite different: 5.8 percent had abortions and 81.5 percent carried to full term. Washington (1982) suggests that the abortion rate for Black teens increased for the period 1973 through 1977 when the federal administration was willing to support legalized abortions. Since 1977, the accessibility of free abortion clinics to many poor Blacks has been severely curtailed. She concludes that: "Black teens come from a cultural ethos that generally disapproves of abortion, and I would speculate that religious beliefs and reverence for life form the bases of these sentiments" (p. 18).

Taborn and Battle (1984) acknowledge that religion, extended-family concepts, and personal perceptions of Blacks create a tendency not to favor abortions. Black human service agencies tend to reinforce the value that abortion is not an acceptable means of coping with Black adolescent pregnancy (Taborn & Battle, 1984).

Human service workers must acknowledge that among Blacks there are some unique, strong, emotionally-laden feelings associated with decisions regarding abortion. It might be more prudent to assume that abortion is generally viewed in negative terms in the Black community. Yet that consequent behavior—participation or nonparticipation in abortion—may be in conflict with both personal and cultural values, for there is increased likelihood of a decision to abort by Black females who are older and/or on a higher socioeconomic level. The awareness of heightened stress while coping with the conflicting values around abortion (regardless of the decision) should form the basis for interventive strategies.

BLACK VIEWS ON FORMAL ADOPTION

Those in the helping professions need to acknowledge that Blacks tend not to approve the placing of their children for formal adoption. There is also a trend for White adolescent mothers who carry their babies to full term to place them for adoption (Scales & Gordon, 1979 as reported in Washington, 1982).

In the Black community, keeping the child is an acceptable, traditional solution to becoming a single parent. Values in the Black community support not disparaging the illegitimate child (Staples, 1971; Furstenberg, 1971; Washington, 1982; and Thompson, 1980). Blacks usually place a high value on having children. As a representative of a large private adoption agency, Sharrar (1971) conducted interviews with Black unwed mothers. Responses to her were sometime hostile, sometimes indifferent. The general result was that the girls were against adoption, along with their having little understanding or interest in the adoptive processes. Festinger (1971) found that unwed Black mothers' opposition to adoption was related to several factors including: their wanting to live independently; a negative view of placement possibilities for the child (Black and interracial children tend *not* to be adopted); mother's background (mothers from single-parent homes are more likely to keep their children); and anticipation of social and emotional support.

Washington (1982) provides a Black cultural perspective by discussing the history of informal adoptive processes commonly practiced in Black communities. She finds anti-adoption views to be consistent with the concept of extended family, collectivism and group survival, as well as a pragmatic response to the problem that Black children tend to be at risk for not being adopted. Taborn and Battle (1984) state:

It is well known, for example, that Black children who are seeking homes through the adoptive process experience great difficulty. While there are literally "waiting lines" of potential adoptive parents for White children, hundreds of thousands of Black children go unadopted each year. (p. 12)

CONCLUSION

It can be seen that Black adolescent females have a relatively high rate of out-of-wedlock childbirth and that the majority are opting to keep their children; these are not new social phenomena. On an increasing basis, White adolescent females are taking the same route and this fact has propelled the issue into the social problem arena, with its concomitant value conflicts about premarital coitus, contraception, abortion, adoption, etc.

This chapter sought to highlight comparative studies, with a focus on unique aspects on pregnancy, etc., as they relate to Blacks. The awareness of uniqueness in these areas for Blacks is important and cautionary, since human service strategies to meet this national problem will in all likelihood be value-focused from the perspective of the majority group. Black and other minority adolescents must be viewed as having some unique social, cultural and psychological needs, and thus they should command alternative interventive strategies that have been for too long designed with the majority group in mind. Washington (1982) discusses the development of new models in Colorado for assisting Black adolescent females. Other attempts are discussed in detail in Taborn and Battle (1984) concerning a program in Minneapolis, Minnesota.

While there is a strong need for Black organizations, scholars, and practitioners to continue to adapt human service programs and interventive strategies to meet the unique needs of Black clients, there is a concurrent need to recognize that Black clients are likely to be serviced by human service workers who represent diverse racial, cultural, economical, and educational backgrounds. This article constitutes an attempt to communicate concerns in the area of Black adolescent parenthood to that broad range of professionals with the hope that they too will contribute to the solution of this problem in a professionally-studied and culturally sensitive manner.

REFERENCES

Bernard, Jessie (1966). *Marriage and family among Negroes*. Englewood Cliffs, New Jersey: Prentice-Hall, Inc.

Butts, J. D. (1981). Adolescent sexuality and teenage pregnancy from a Black perspective. In T. Odoms (Ed.), *Teenage pregnancy in a family context*. Philadelphia: Temple University.

Chilman, D. (1978). *Adolescent sexuality in a changing American society*. Washington, DC: U.S. Department of Health, Education and Welfare.

de'Anda, D. (1983). Pregnancy in early and late adolescence. *Journal of Youth and Adolescence, 12*(1) 33-42.

Festinger, T. B. (1971). Unwed mothers and their decisions to keep or surrender children. *Child Welfare, 50*(5), 253-263.

Finkel, M. L. & Finkel D. J. (1978). Male adolescent contraceptive utilization. *Adolescence, 13*(51), 443-451.

Furstenberg, Frank F. (1971). Birth control experience among pregnant adolescents: The process of unplanned parenthood. *Social Problems, 19*(2), 192-203.

Guttmacher Institute (1976). *11 million teenagers*. New York: Alan Guttmacher Institute.

Held, Linda (1981). Self-esteem and social network of the young pregnant teenager. *Adolescence, 14*(64), 905-910.

Hendricks, Leo E. & Fullilove, Robert E. (1983). Locus of control and use of contraception among unmarried Black adolescent fathers and their controls: A preliminary report. *Journal of Youth and Adolescence, 12*(3), 225-233.

James, W. F., James, P. & Walker, E. (1977). Some problems of sexual growth in adolescent underprivileged unwed Black girls. *Journal of the National Medical Association, 69*(9), 631-633.

Jessor, S. & Jessor, R. (1975). Transition from virginity to nonvirginity among youth: A social-psychological study over time. *Developmental Psychology, 4*, 473-484.

Johnson, Carla L. (1972). *Premarital sex and family planning attitudes: A report of a pilot study in rural Georgia county*. Washington, DC: U.S. Department of Health, Education and Welfare, Social and Rehabilitation Service.

Namerow, P. B. & Jones, J. E. (1982). Ethnic variation in adolescent use of a contraceptive service. *Journal of Adolescent Health Care, 3*(3), 165-172.

Presser, Harriet B. (1978). Age at menarche, socio-sexual behavior. *Social Biology, 25*(2), 94-101.

Roebuck, J. & McGee, M. (1977). Attitudes toward premarital sex and sexual behavior among Black high school girls. *Journal of Sex Research, 13*(2), 104-114.

Rosen, R. R. (1980). Adolescent pregnancy decision-making: Are parents important? *Adolescence, 15*(57), 43-53.

Scales, P. & Gordon, S. (1979). Preparing today's youth for tomorrow's family: Recommendations of the Wing-Spread Conference on Early Adolescent Sexuality and Health Care,

June 3-5, 1979, Impact '79. *Journal of the Institute for Family Research and Education* *1*(2), 3-8.

Semens, J. P. & Lainers, W. M., Jr. (1968). *Teenage Pregnancy*. Springfield, Illinois: Charles C Thomas.

Sharrar, M. L. (1971). Attitude of Black natural parents regarding adoption. *Child Welfare,* *50*(5), 286-289.

Smith, P. B., Weinman, M. L. & Mumford, D. M. (1982). Social affective factors associated with adolescent pregnancy. *Journal of School Health, 52*(2), 90-93.

Staples, R. (1971). Toward sociology of the Black family: A theoretical and methodological assessment. *Journal of Marriage and the Family, 33,* 119-138.

Taborn, J. M. & Battle, S. F. (1984). *Black adolescent parenthood: A manual for human service practitioners*. Minneapolis: Survival Skills Institutes, Inc.

Thompson, K. S. (1980). A comparison of Black and White adolescents' beliefs about having children. *Journal of Marriage and the Family, 2*(1), 133-139.

U.S. Department of Health, Education and Welfare (1973). *Age at menarche: United States vital and health statistics*. Series 11, No. 133, Washington, DC: Government Printing Office.

Vadies E. & Hale, D. (1977). Attitudes of adolescent males toward abortion, contraception and sexuality. *Social Work in Health Care, 3*(2), 169-174.

Vincent, Clark E. (1961). *Unmarried mothers*. New York: Free Press of Glencoe.

Washington, Anita C. (1982). A cultural and historical perspective on pregnancy-related activity among U.S. teenagers. *Journal of Black Psychology, 9*(1), 1-28

Zelnik, M. & Kantner, J. F. (1977). Sexual and contraceptive experiences of young unmarried women in the United States, 1971 and 1976. *Family Planning Perspectives, 9*(2), 55-71.

Zelnik, M. & Kantner, J. F. (1979). Reasons for non-use of contraception by sexually active women aged 15-19. *Family Planning Perspectives, 11*(5), 289-296.

Zelnik, M. & Kantner, J. F. (1980). Sexual activity among metropolitan-area teenagers: 1971-1979. *Family Planning Perspectives, 12*(5), 230-237.

Black Adolescent Pregnancy:
A Literature Review

Donna L. Franklin

ABSTRACT. Adolescent childbearing and parenthood are growing phenomena in this society, which has given rise to an increased concern and a concomitant proliferation in the literature. This chapter examines studies that have endeavored to identify the causes and consequences of adolescent pregnancy. Special attention is given to those studies that have evaluated the influences of race and socioeconomic class in that higher rates of out-of-wedlock births to adolescents are found among lower-income Blacks. While the literature is in theoretical disarray, this chapter identifies five primary explanatory theories and organizes these studies by linking them to one of these theoretical frameworks. The discussion delineates the conceptual strengths and weaknesses of these studies in explaining the race- and class-specific aspects of the problem, and explores implications for intervention.

Adolescent pregnancy and parenting are seriously growing phenomena in our society. Increased public concern embraces some programmatic development as well as a proliferation in the literature of human service professionals. Indeed the causes and consequences of teenage pregnancy and parenting warrant sound theorizing that can lead to more sensitive, constructive intervention with adolescents and their families.

Yet many studies about adolescent pregnancy seem to circumvent the concerns of race, gender, and socioeconomic class. This avoidance can be harmful if it contributes to biased assumptions and programs that fail to meet the needs of Black adolescents . . . especially when higher rates of births by unwed adolescents are found among lower-income Black youth.

Donna L. Franklin, MSW, PhD, is an assistant professor at the University of Chicago, School of Social Service Administration. She is currently a co-investigator on a major research project that focuses on urban poverty and family structure. Her primary research interests are how social and structural processes interact to influence an adolescent female's decisions regarding sexuality and pregnancy.

15

The literature appears to be fragmented and theoretically scattered. Five primary explanatory theories are examined in this chapter; further studies are linked to one of these theoretical frameworks. The discussion sets out the conceptual strengths and weaknesses of these studies in terms of how they address — or do not address — race- and class-specific aspects of adolescent pregnancy, as well as attempting to delineate implications for sensitized, pragmatic intervention.

Adolescent out-of-wedlock pregnancies have been studied extensively from demographic and ecological perspectives. While considerable controversy exists about the relationship between numerical and proportionate increases in adolescent pregnancies, developments in the Black community around this issue warrant special attention. For example, by the end of the 1950s, only 15 percent of all births were to unwed Black women. By 1978, the percentage had grown to 53 percent, a figure six times greater than for Whites (National Center for Health Statistics, 1981). Significantly, during the twenty-year span from 1947 to 1967, births to unwed Black women increased 106.3 percent (Bernard, 1966). Age is a factor in these out-of-wedlock statistics: In 1978 about 1.2 percent of White teenagers and 9.2 of Black teenagers gave birth outside of marriage. More strikingly, 83 percent of the births to Black teenagers and 29 percent of those to White teenagers were to unmarried adolescents (National Center for Health Statistics, 1978).

As the antecedent to pregnancy, sexual activity is germane to the discussion of adolescent pregnancies. According to Zelnik and Kantner (1977), racial differences exist in incidence of sexual intercourse and in contraceptive use. For example, Black teenagers were more than twice as likely to have sexual intercourse than were White teenagers (62.7 percent versus 30.8 percent), and Black women tended to initiate their sexual careers at an earlier age (15.6 versus 16.3 years). On the other hand, White teenagers were twice as likely as Black teenagers to use contraceptives at each act of intercourse (Shah, Zelnik & Kantner, 1975). Consequently, 27 percent of the Black teenagers in their study reported being or having been pregnant, compared to 9.3 percent of the White teens interviewed. When Zelnik & Kantner (1980) repeated their survey of young women between the ages of fifteen and nineteen, they found that the use of contraceptives had increased for both races, and the gap between the races was narrowing in regard to sexual activity as well.

The increase in the rate of out-of-wedlock births corresponds closely to the rise of female-headed families. The number of families headed by women grew 51 percent during the 1970s. Families headed by White women increased by 42.1 percent, for Black women by 72.9 percent (U.S. Bureau of Census, Current Population Reports, 1980). In turn, the increase in female-headed families contributes to welfare dependence, which is fostered in a number of ways for adolescent mothers. Their lack of education particularly (Card & Wise, 1978; Moore & Hofferth, 1977; Furstenberg, 1976) is directly related to their lower earnings and greater job dissatisfaction. Moore and Cardwell (1976) estimated that about 60 percent of children born outside of marriage receive welfare, and they reported that "more than half of all AFDC assistance in 1975 was paid to women who were or had been teenage mothers."

Although no nationwide studies have adequately examined variables of race and class associated with adolescent fertility, a few regional studies have been performed. These studies suggest that racism and poverty do interact, thereby contributing to limited educational and occupational opportunities and to deteriorating family relations (Kantner & Zelnik, 1972; Jessor & Jessor, 1975; Chilman, 1978). Numerous empirical studies have examined correlates of adolescent pregnancy, yet few are linked to any theoretical framework. Hence, a problem so complex requires not only examination of the impact of race and class, but should expand to looking at possible explanatory theories about how race, class, and sexual expression interact. Understanding causal phenomena can be the first step in developing effective interventions. Thus this chapter explores a number of theories which seek to explain adolescent sexuality, pregnancy, and childbearing. The conceptual strengths and weaknesses of these theories are reviewed in light of race and class aspects of the problem of adolescent pregnancy. It is difficult to comprehend fully the significance of the increasingly emerging familial form in the Black community of female-headed intergenerational families without simultaneously addressing the unique dimension of Black women's experiences in this society. The exclusion of the variables of gender and race from discussions of adolescent pregnancy not only influences the questions that are asked and how they are answered but those questions left out altogether. Interpretations of subsequent research findings are affected and their utility is weakened. Thus the evaluation of these causal theories and their application for helpful intervention must permit examining how racial, gender and class differences affect understanding adolescent childbearing and parenting.

ACCESS TO KNOWLEDGE APPROACH

The access to knowledge approach to looking at adolescent sex and childbearing has to its advantage a relatively common-sense view of cause and a relatively simple solution (at least technically). This theory asserts that, on one hand, adolescents are increasingly sexually active because they have more awareness of and knowledge about sex — at least its mechanics — as well as a notion of its importance in our culture's view of love and romance. Also they have increased opportunities for indulging in sex. On the other hand, adolescents become pregnant because they lack knowledge of the mechanics of conception and contraception, and lack easy access to reliable, inexpensive methods of birth control.

The proposed solution to the problem based on this reasoning is a two-pronged attack: Increase accurate information regarding conception and contraception, and increase the availability of contraceptive devices to adolescents.

Joseph Califano, a recent director of the Department of Health and Human Services described in 1978 the trends in teen pregnancy as "a national epidemic which the federal government must address" and called for action consistent with the access to knowledge approach. The proposed thrust of this public policy was to increase access to contraceptives by teenagers. Interestingly, Mr. Califano's assessment reflected his lack of familiarity with past federal policies and their minuscule effects on the problem!

Programs to Increase Knowledge

The 1960s witnessed increased interest in adolescent pregnancy as a social problem. The legal status of the child and concomitant moral dilemmas no longer concerned social planners as much as did the contribution of adolescent parenthood to the poverty cycle. Redefining adolescent pregnancy in economic terms yielded federally-financed medical and family planning programs which were targeted especially for adolescents. Black adolescents were identified as "high risk" in that they had higher birthrates and studies confirmed the heavier consequences accruing to this group. Subsequently, disproportionate amounts of federal dollars were channeled into the Black community, providing inner-city women and teens with hospital and clinic-based perinatal care, sex education, and contraception. Blacks responded by charging the federal government with intent to commit genocide on residents of the Black community (Yette, 1971).

The result of this massive national effort to decrease the adolescent birthrate was in reality underutilization of these services by women. Ten-year follow-up studies of these public services demonstrated that inaccessibility to contraceptives and abortion were but two small factors contributing to adolescent pregnancy and parenthood (Greer & Lesniak, 1979). Even when contraceptive services to adolescents were exemplary, pregnancy rates did not decline (Shearer & Shearer, 1979). Few adolescents requested contraceptive services, and only limited gains were made in lowering health risks for pregnant teenagers, young mother, and their babies (Jekel, Harrison, Bancroft, Tyler & Klerman, 1975).

However, a program conducted in the private sector with government funds had more successful results. A model program based upon assumptions of lack of knowledge and lack of access as primary causes of adolescent pregnancy has been operating in selected public school clinics in St. Paul, Minnesota since 1973. The clinics offer a wide range of adolescent health care services, including contraceptive services, venereal disease testing and treatment, and other ancillary services. The program attracted a sizable proportion of each school's population, and the percentage of female students using contraceptive services in the school clinics increased to 25 percent in the 1977-78 school year. Fertility rates at the schools dropped substantially (52 percent over 3 years in the junior-senior high school; 23 percent over 3 years in the two high schools). Program staff members attribute their success largely to the accessibility of free and confidential services, including educational and social services given prior to medical encounters (Edwards, Steinman, Arnold & Hakanson, 1980). It should be noted that programs of this kind in inner-city high schools in the biggest American cities have not met with comparable success.

Studies present conflicting evidence regarding the effectiveness of increasing access to information and it is hoped decreasing rates of teenage pregnancy and childbearing. For instance, Zelnik and Kantner (1977), as well as Finkel and Finkel (1975), found small positive correlations between sex education and knowledge, while

Goldsmith, Gabrielson, and Gabrielson (1972) found no evidence of such a correlation. Further, Evans, Selstad and Welcher (1976) found that knowledge of contraceptive methods increased over time with counseling, and Reichelt and Werley (1975) reported a "striking improvement" in knowledge of all areas of birth control methods following a single clinic rap session.

One explanation for such disparate findings is the variance in definitions of "sex education" and "counseling" which can vary widely in content and quality of execution. Proponents of sex education are acutely aware of such variability but tend to assert that any sex education is better than none at all. One unequivocal finding in the literature is a positive relationship between age and knowledge of conception and contraception. One might argue that this reflects increased chances that come with age of exposure to information and experience. However, there are arguments that this relationship suggests instead a maturational factor, that is, appropriate assimilation of information is contingent upon a certain level of maturity or cognitive development. This perspective will be presented in greater detail later in this chapter.

Findings from investigations focusing on knowledge of and access to contraception have contributed minimally to our understanding the complex issue of adolescent pregnancy; they have done even less to enhance our understanding of this most critical problem in poor Black communities. Earlier studies reported that lack of knowledge concerning contraception or the lack of access to it was not etiologically significant in lower-income Black communities (Furie, 1966; Lee & Temerlin, 1964; Rains, 1971; Schofield, 1965).

Ladner (1971) countered these findings when she observed that misinformation was disseminated to adolescents via their mothers and grandmothers regarding the various methods of contraception. She states that "folk tradition acts to perpetuate the process of misinformation and consequent non-usage of contraceptives" (p. 253). Hence individuals who attempt to provide knowledge to this target population would be advised to broaden their intervention to include the adolescents' parents. Cultural variations should also be considered. As Fox (1979) suggests:

> Policies that ignore the familial context of teenage sexual behavior, that fail to discern and enlist the familial support based of the teenager, and that undermine rather than supplement the

efforts and effectiveness of parents are likely to yield programs that are wasteful, inefficient and ineffective. (p. 36)

ADOLESCENT COGNITIVE DEVELOPMENT APPROACH

This perspective suggests that for adolescents to make use of available contraceptives, they must anticipate sexual encounters, curb their impulses, seek out needed information, and apply this information to their own behavior. These activities then require formal cognitive operations whereby adolescents can hypothesize abstractly on the consequences of behavior; they can evaluate consequences; and they can trace action to bring about the preferred outcome. It is the developmental task of adolescents to forge their identities and according to Piaget (1952), they are experiencing a shift from concrete to formal operational thought.

An individual capable of concrete operations can only represent cognitively what exists in reality; hypothetical events cannot be easily understood or represented mentally. This limitation colors the meaning of menstruation, conception, and childbirth because the internal physiological processes associated with these experience cannot be imagined in the same way that a person in the formal operations stage imagines them. Consequently, a cognitive development approach suggests that recognition of the risk of pregnancy as the outcome of unprotected sexual intercourse depends upon the adolescent's attaining the stage of formal operational thought and being able to move beyond adolescent egocentrism, that is, being immersed in oneself almost to the exclusion of all else.

One of the consequences of adolescent egocentrism is the adolescent's feeling of being "on stage." Adolescents can spend a great deal of time constructing an imaginary audience, and they envision that the audience "knows" what the thinker knows and is as self-critical as the thinker is (Elkind, 1967). This may account for adolescents' common desire for privacy and their fear that everyone will know about their sexual activity and use of birth control.

Another aspect of this egocentrism is developing a personal fable or a construction complementary to the imaginary audience (Elkind, 1967). Adolescents see themselves as being so important to so many people (in the imaginary audience) that they come to regard themselves as special and unique, so much so that no one else could know how they feel or experience what they experience.

Further, the personal fable contributes to a sense of invincibility: "unfortunate things may happen to others, but I'm different" (Elkind, 1967). The thousands of pregnant adolescents who think they can have intercourse and not get pregnant operate with personal fables.

Researched evidence concerning Piaget's theory of cognitive development suggests that not only is formal operational thought a phenomenon quite distinct from concrete operational thought, but also suggests repeated demonstrations of age-related improvements in formal thought during adolescence (Neimark, 1975). On the other hand, research evidence also points out that formal reasoning is only one style of mature thinking (Dulit, 1972; Elkind, 1975). The extent to which any individual develops and utilizes formal thought depends on cultural influences, schooling, and individual experiences, and perhaps less on innate developmental processes. Environmental factors may influence the utilization of formal operations as much as cognitive development.

This position clearly carries implications for understanding the differential effects of the inner-city environment on its residents. How this environment impacts on the particular stages of cognitive development has been addressed in the literature (Broen, 1972; Blake, 1979; Holt, 1972). One can conclude from these studies that inner-city adolescents are probably more susceptible to psychological "errors" or vulnerabilities in formal thought during their teenage years.

While this perspective is not extremely helpful in suggesting interventive strategies to alleviate the growth of adolescent pregnancy, it becomes clearer that the inner-city adolescent is especially vulnerable during this transitional period in cognitive development. The probability of getting through this period unscathed is therefore diminished by the adolescent's cognitive capacities. If cognitive development and increased access to knowledge are put into perspective for adolescents, how does an adolescent's social schema impact decisions and actions concerning sexuality and the risk of getting pregnant?

SOCIAL INFLUENCE APPROACH

Adolescents are typically seen as rejecting adult or parental values and norms while rigidly conforming to the dictates of peer culture. If the peer culture dictates sex, most adolescents will comply.

The sign of impending contagion is the phrase, "But everyone else is. . . ." The implicit causal explanations can be generally characterized as social influence or reference group theories, and they happen to occupy a central place in social science, particularly in the field of social psychology.

One of the fundamental, cherished principles of the social sciences is that individuals are greatly influenced by membership in various social groups, whether family, neighborhood, or work. The prevailing generalization is that preadolescent and adolescent children are continuously moving away from parents and toward peers as a primary reference group. However, does this reflect Black teens? A cursory look at research on the Black family seems in order.

During the mid-1960s, numerous studies were produced that examined the cumulative effects of racial isolation and class subordination on behavioral patterns in urban lower-income communities. Clark (1965) and Rainwater (1966) portrayed the destructive features of urban ghetto life. They also comprehensively analyzed structural conditions that, combined with a race-specific experiences, were assumed to produce behavioral norms that may be characterized as "self-perpetuating pathology" (Clark, 1965). Restricted access to or exclusion from stable, high-status employment, and from equitable participation in the majority culture helped to undermine the fabric of Black family life, according to this view.

Rainwater's tangled thesis about pathology asserted that the disorganized, less competent family in turn inculcated in its members attitudes, behaviors, and values that restrict their ability to be upwardly mobile and to adapt effectively to the general society. Consistent with prevailing sociological perspectives of the time and borrowing from Sutherland's concept of "differential association," Vincent (1961) asserted that sexual behavior was learned through identification and interaction within intimate personal groups. What about family influence?

A more recent study conducted by Hogan and Kitagawa (1982) looked at correlates of fertility among Black adolescents. They found that family socioeconomic background, and parent and sibling fertility patterns strongly affected adolescents' attitudes. Other support comes from the study conducted by Yankelovich (1969) when he reported that 75 percent of his adolescent sample said they accepted and agreed with their parents' values.

Parental communication about sex may forestall or postpone a child's sexual activity (see Fox, 1979). Parental expression about contraception seems related to encouraging more effective contraceptive use by daughters (Furstenberg, 1976; Miller, 1976). Other variables related to sexual and contraceptive behavior reflected parent-child relations: happiness of the parental home; closeness to mother; parents sexual knowledge; parental power structures and domestic division of labor; mother's participation in the labor force; the family's socioeconomic status; and size of the family. While other studies seem to lean toward the continuing stronger orientation of adolescents toward peers (Costanzo & Shaw, 1966; Berndt, 1979; Curtis, 1975), Brittain proposed twenty years ago a situational hypothesis as explanation for the apparent discrepancy between parental or peer reference for teens (1963). Adolescents, in his view, refer to peers in situations that have implications for current status and identity, and to parents when future (adult) status and roles are involved.

For inner-city adolescents, however, this view does not permit many options. If they turn to their parents who may be unemployed and receiving welfare assistance, and who may have been adolescent parents themselves, they are not provided with models of viable alternatives to sexual activity that may lead to pregnancy. On the other hand, if they turn to their peers, many of whom are already adolescent parents, positive role models are not available there either. Subsequently, a sense of hopelessness can be perpetuated from both sides. Fischman and Palley (1978) support this perspective for they view conception as stemming from the adolescent female's realization of her slim chances for educational and career achievement. This results in compensatory enhancement of precocious sexual fulfillment, pregnancy, and ultimately parenthood. Goldfarb et al. (1977) likewise found an association between poor school performance and vulnerability to becoming pregnant.

Thompson and Spanier (1978) drew an empirically-based map of social influences upon the use of contraception by undergraduate females, and they found parental influences on contraceptive use by either men or women to be minimal. Persuasion by one's partner to use contraception emerged as the most powerful influence on the use of contraception by both men and women.

Among females, emotional involvement with a partner enhances the partner's influence over using contraceptives. Sexual exclusivity and frequency of intercourse are also factors. Also for women, influence of friends to use contraceptives contributes significantly to effective contraceptive use; women seem more vulnerable to friends' influence than males do. The influence of a partner and one's friends are negatively related: If a woman is deeply involved with her partner, his influence regarding contraceptive use is likely predominant, otherwise, she is more inclined to depend on her friends for contraceptive support.

This study by Thompson and Spanier (1978) has some important implications for research on adolescent fertility patterns among Black lower-income groups. Although this study did not control for the variables of race or class in the respondent population, it did look at both male and female relationships. Most previous studies of this kind overlooked Black males. Proceeding on the "matriarchal hypothesis," they assume that Black males are either absent in these relationships, or if present, only tangentially involved in the lives of these Black females.

While small regional surveys have been conducted on Black adolescent males to explore their attitudes on contraception, abortion, etc. (Hendricks, 1982; Johnson & Staples, 1976), their influence on the Black adolescent female's decision to get pregnant has not been addressed. Other studies have investigated conjugal decision-making and dominance patterns, controlling for the variables of race and class, and these findings may have implications for the adolescent pregnancy dilemma. Studies conducted by Hyman and Reed (1969), Cromwell and Cromwell (1978), and Hammond and Enoch (1976) suggest that Black male-female dominance in biparental families is curvilinear, that is, related to the man's employment status. These studies sampled only legally married couples with "working" males. Therefore, inference cannot be made to families where unemployment is an endemic and a chronic problem.

In a more complex and elaborately designed survey study, Tenhouten (1970) compared 550 Black and White, low and middle socioeconomic status, biparental families in terms of conjugal power (i.e., male dominance ideology, conjugal decision-making power, and conjugal power structure) and parental power (i.e., mother's parental power, mother's and father's parent-child decision power and parental control). Results showed that wife-dominated families were generally infrequent and were least frequent in Black, lower-class families in terms of conjugal power. There were distinct social class connections to maternal power, that is, low-socioeconomic status mothers were more powerful in this dimension, although Black women were slightly more powerful than White women.

These studies tend to support this researcher's clinical observations regarding the involvement of the Black male in the decision-making process in the Black underclass household or relationship. The involvement of Black males needs to be evaluated more precisely for it may shed new light on understanding the Black adolescent female's vulnerability to early pregnancy especially in lower-income families.

PSYCHOLOGICAL APPROACH

One reason given for why increased knowledge of and access to contraceptives fails to stem teenage pregnancies can be attributed to conscious or unconscious motivations to become pregnant. Character deficits are perceived in the adolescent's personality or in the psychodynamics of the adolescent's family relationships. Consider the description of the "self-picture" painted by pregnant adolescents studied by Zongker (1977):

> . . . they had pervasive feelings of being "bad", dissatisfied with their own behavior, intense doubts about their identity and only nominal feelings of self-worth. The subjects were defensive, unhappy with the relationships that they had both with their family and with society in general and basically overwhelmed by feelings of low self-esteem. They were poorly integrated as persons, possessed a deficit of adequate coping behaviors and exhibited a high degree of instability and conflict. (p. 480)

Several strands of psychological theorizing can be distinguished in this description, and they have been addressed by different studies. The first characterizes sexually active and/or pregnant teenagers as suffering some personality deficit, whether it be poor personality integration, inadequate coping skills, a high degree of psychic conflict, and/or instability (Zongker, 1977). A lack of social maturity and responsibility and impulsivity has been observed by Rovinsky (1972), and Pannor (1971), and powerlessness or external locus of control by Bauman and Udry (1972), and MacDonald (1970). Findings from other studies (Jessor & Jessor, 1975; Cvetkovich, Grote, Lieberman & Miller, 1978) suggest that, particularly for girls, strong dependency needs and the desire for affection and improved self-esteem lead to intercourse.

Kaplan, Smith, and Pokorny (1979), in a rare longitudinal study of an entire high school population, found that pregnant adolescents were more likely than their peers to have had devaluating experiences attributed to parents, teachers, or peers. Such experiences result in a negative self-attitude which teens attempt to reverse by rejecting the evaluative and normative structure espoused and controlled by parents, teachers, or peers. Combined with exposure to and positive evaluation of deviant activities, the likelihood increases that these teens will engage in activities that may include premarital sex and childbearing.

Yet another strand of psychological theorizing focuses on deficits in familial relations. Sexual behaviors and pregnancy are interpreted as rebellion against parents who are too strict or as attempts to evoke attention and concern from permissive or indifferent parents. Sexual intimacy and possible a baby might fill an emotional gap left by rejecting parents. Zongker (1977) explains the greater prevalence of adolescent pregnancies by pointing to households where fathers are absent. Utilizing a psychoanalytic perspective, he asserts: "The traditional psychoanalytic view concludes that deprivation of a male parental relationship within the family impels a daughter toward seeking compensatory masculine attention, as through sexual behavior" (p. 486).

A major problem with many of these studies based on the psychological model is that they tend to be more descriptive in nature than explanatory. They often use nonrandom samples, drawing upon their own experiences with pregnant girls who have been referred for psychiatric or psychotherapeutic services. In spite of these limitations, these perspectives correspond quite closely to findings in studies conducted on Black respondents. For example, Ladner (1972) described early psychosexual development as an experience which provides girls with a sense of "belonging and of feeling needed by their boyfriends . . . a sense of identity and utility" (p. 209). While her participant-observation and case study approach seems vulnerable to investigator bias and cannot be generalized beyond her sample, her data still provides important insight into the internal dynamics of lower-income Black women and their adaptation to unhealthy environmental conditions.

Ladner further enhances our understanding of a study conducted on fertility patterns of public assistance recipients in California (Keefe, 1983). Keefe's data suggest that the fertility behavior of women already on public assistance did not seem to be motivated by economic considerations, as many observers had assumed. Many of these women chose to become pregnant because they believed a tenuous relationship with a man would become more permanent and stable if she bore his child. Most investigators have not evaluated this critical dimension of the Black women's psychosexual dilemma, that is, her emotional vulnerability to the Black man.

Environment and the Psychological Approach

The weakest aspect of the psychological model clearly is its failure to take into account the influence of environment. Research studies that have taken this variable into account have found that poverty often breeds attitudes of fatalism, powerlessness, alienation, hopelessness and a sense of personal incompetence, particularly with respect to striving for long-range educational and occupational goals (Stack, 1974; Rainwater, 1966; Rubin, 1976).

The influences of the socioeconomic variables of poverty status, family income, and parental education have been found to contribute to racial differentials in experience with coitus. The higher the socioeconomic level, the lower the proportion with sexual experience. For Whites, the effect is rather slight. Among Blacks, the effect is considerably stronger. Except where the male parent has a college degree, Black-White differences prevail (Kantner & Zelnik, 1972). Given the relative importance of a father's funneling instrumental benefits to family members, this model would consistently predict a higher incidence of sexual activity and pregnancy among adolescents in female-headed households.

Black History and the Psychological Approach

The historical dimension of environmental constraints is often overlooked. The exploitation of Black women has become a permanent feature in American social and economic life, in that Black women in terms of their self-esteem and competence have been assaulted as workers, as Blacks, and as women. Black men have also suffered, and this has been exacerbated by their inability to protect their women and families from this assault and exploitation. The impact of these experiences is immeasurable and historically has increased tensions between the sexes in the Black community (Giddings, 1984). While these dynamics are complex, they may contain clues to understanding the Black woman's need for a sense of belonging and identity that is often attained in the context of stable male-female relationships.

The awareness of this need for a low-income Black female may begin during prepubescence when she realizes that such relationships may not be available to her. Personality and social theories have explored these developmental issues within the context of the social environment. In Mead's (1934) sociological concept of self, he stresses the development of the self as the result of interaction between the unique "I" — the individual — and the "me" — the reflection for the larger society — which Mead calls the "generalized other." One of Adler's (1956) central ideas supports this relationship between the self and the environment. He proposed that personality develops in one's moving toward a better adaptation to the social and physical environment. Thus as the Black lower-income female becomes aware of her socioeconomic status and that of her male peers, she perceives she does not have opportunities for traditional marriage and family, vis-a-vis Black males' restricted access to jobs. In addition, she recognizes her own limitations in achieving socioeconomic or career success. How she handles this sense of hopelessness and futility can usually be gauged by the availability and strengths of her family or social support networks. Soloman (1976) discusses the strength of the family and/or group ties which she refers to as the "benevolent circle," and she argues this can serve as a buttress against the impact of negative valuations from the larger society.

The psychological models assert that the underlying causes of teenage sexuality and childbearing are troubled personality characteristics arising from pathological and/or maladaptive familial relationships. By locating cause in the individual or her family, this approach is susceptible to charges of blaming the victim.

Psychological theories propose that some form of psychotherapy and/or family therapy can ameliorate the consequences of psychological maladaptation or — at an earlier stage — can serve to prevent or remedy patterns in familial interactions that might result in psychological maladaptation. Such interventive methods are relatively costly, time-consuming, and available to only a small percentage of the adolescents and their families who may need such service. Further, the literature reveals that long-term psychodynamic, insight-

oriented therapies are generally viewed by mental health professionals as ineffective in treating the lower socioeconomic status client
who has many other problems as well (Garfield, 1971; Lee & Temerlin, 1970). These groups even when mobilized to "do something about their problems," have higher attrition and discontinu-
ance rates in psychotherapy when compared to middle-income
groups (Fiester & Rudestam, 1974; Craig & Huffine, 1976). The
efficacy of therapy may be debatable then for Black adolescents
who are faced with many economic and/or family stressors.

DECISION-MAKING APPROACH: A MULTIVARIATE ANALYSIS

The review of the literature up to this point suggests that adolescent pregnancy cannot be explained by any single approach, although each makes some contribution to our understanding of this
complex phenomenon. Each perspective tends to be reductionistic
in that it either explains adolescent pregnancy by looking at the
individual adolescent's characteristics, *or* from the social environment, *or* the distribution of resources perspective. All these models
are basically univariate in their approach. It is quite clear from
studying the literature that not only are the causes of adolescent
sexuality and pregnancy multiple, but there is also overlap in explanatory frameworks. What is needed is a multivariate approach
that would identify the independent contribution of the variables
within these frameworks.

A research design generally characterized as a decision-making
approach would meet these requirements. This approach perceives
adolescents acting upon their incipient sexuality as a conscious decision, that is, adolescents have weighed the costs and benefits of
the alternatives available to them. The critical factor in using such
an approach is not what the actual probabilities of the costs and
benefits are, but how aggregate respondent populations perceive
consequences of their decisions. The influence of race and social
class needs to be evaluated within this framework.

What are the options available to adolescents when they consider
engaging in sexual activity with members of the opposite sex? Decisions involve assessing the probability and relative significance of
consequences such as (1) an out-of-wedlock birth; (2) loss of opportunities for achieving educational, occupational, and marital goals;

(3) the financial costs of childrearing; (4) the psychic, social, and financial costs of abortion; (5) the psychic and social rewards of parenthood; and (6) impact on relationships with parents, peers, or partners. Ajzen and Fishbein (1980) delineate this approach when they state:

> Basic to this approach is the view that people use the information available to them in a reasonable manner to arrive at their decisions. This is not to say that their behavior will always be reasonable or appropriate from an objective point of view. People's information is often incomplete and at times also incorrect. But we would argue that a person's behavior follows quite logically and systematically from whatever information he happens to have available. (p. 244)

The decision-making model utilizes personality characteristics, demographic variables, and social factors only as external variables that influence the beliefs a person holds or the relative importance attached to attitudinal and normative factors.

Using a costs and benefits analytic model, White (1979) made predictions regarding out-of-wedlock pregnancy. He assumed that decisions regarding out-of-wedlock childbearing related to the perceived costs. For example, though most unmarried mothers eventually marry (93 percent of Whites and 81 percent of Blacks by age 45), out-of-wedlock childbearing may motivate women to "settle" for less desirable marriages. However, the cost of unwed pregnancy depends on the nature of the marriage market as adolescents who are contemplating engaging in intercourse perceive it. The quality of the marriage market, in turn, depends on the availability of eligible males and the economic viability of marriage as measured by male unemployment rates.

On both counts, the marital opportunities for Black females, whether mothers or not, are inferior to those for White females, since the ratio of males to females is lower, and the unemployment rates for males are higher for Blacks than for Whites. Hence, the marriage opportunity cost of unwed births could rationally be calculated as lower for Black females than for White females.

On the benefit side, evidence indicates that children are more highly valued by Blacks than by Whites for both intrinsic and instrumental reasons. Thompson (1980) reports on a high school survey of the perceived value of children of Black and White adolescents. He found significant differences by race and sex, 36 percent and 27 percent, respectively, of the total variance in valuations. That is, Blacks were more likely than Whites, and males more likely than females to agree that having children promotes marital success, personal security and approval from others, and that having children is highly creative, pleasurable, and emotionally satisfying to both mothers and fathers. In two questions regarding the contribution of children to personal satisfaction and fatherly pride, Blacks responded more eagerly than Whites. Thompson concludes that "Black youths anticipate the having of a child (especially a son) as more of a special and important event than do White adolescents" (p. 138).

These findings are consistent with Stack's (1974) sample of low-income Black females. Her data indicated that children serve an important function in expanding kinship networks of mutual assistance. This is, even if the parents of a baby do not marry, the father's family usually assumes a share of the responsibility not only for the baby but for the baby's mother and her family. Further, Testa (1983) asserts that the strong value placed on children may explain why more Black families than White tend to provide assistance to the unwed mother. His research found that 70 percent of his low-income adolescent Black respondents were living at home with their parents, compared with 44 percent of Whites and Hispanics in the same socioeconomic group.

Similarly, the costs of raising a child in a single-mother household will be perceived as relatively high only if marriage can guarantee increased support. This, in turn, depends on the levels of support for married versus unmarried mothers, and the permanence of marriage. White (1979) suggests that the economic opportunity cost of out-of-wedlock pregnancy will be perceived as greatest when employment and wages of potential husbands are high; least when female wages and AFDC support rates compare favorably with support by potential husbands; and less when high rates of divorce, separation or desertion are evident. Again, Black and low-income females might reasonably be expected to discount the economic costs of unwed pregnancy, since opportunities for economically stable husbands are severely limited, and marriage—even if it is stable and enduring—provides less economic benefit than it would for Whites and middle-class females.

A third cost of out-of-wedlock pregnancy is the disruption of usual activities, especially the continuation of schooling and labor force participation by the mother. White (1979) suggests that the cost is perceived as greater when education is considered "important" for women, and where women's labor force participation and their wages are high. The calculation of this cost then is affected by the women's position in the opportunity structure of the society, by sex role expectations which define what is important for women, and by discrimination against women — particularly Black and lower-class women — in education and in the labor force.

White argues that the individual woman will base her decisions on her perception of the opportunities available to women in her community. "Thus, young women who are themselves not in the labor force or married form judgments or accept the judgments of their community about the opportunities which the economy and marriage offer them" (p. 718). Looking at aggregate data for 90 urban locations, White examined the relationships between out-of-wedlock birthrates and his various cost factors. He found that marriage market variables were not significantly related to unwed birthrates, nor were median female earnings. The psychological theorist would counter these findings by arguing that these decisions may not consciously be made by these respondents. Also AFDC rates were negatively related to out-of-wedlock birthrates, which supports Keefe's (1983) findings. He found the predicted relations between out-of-wedlock birthrates and school attendance rates by females as well as labor force participation rates for females, negatively related to out-of-wedlock pregnancies. These findings support data presented earlier in this chapter (Fischman & Palley, 1978; Goldfarb, 1977).

Keefe's model (1983) explains other data as well, including findings by Shaw, Zelnik, and Kantner (1975) that girls with higher educational aspirations were less likely to get pregnant intentionally or to be unconcerned about possible pregnancies, and more likely always to use contraceptives.

The finding that young men are more likely than young women to perceive children as being greater personal and social assets prompts the question of whether females are pressured by males into having children. Also the question that has not been addressed is the male's perception of having children when his life chances of employment are limited and constricted. That is, does he like the female view children as a way of enhancing his self-esteem, thereby causing him to place more pressure on the female. The employment issue certainly has important implications in the Black community in that over 50 percent of inner-city youth are unemployed and the proportion of Black teenage males who have never held a job increased from 32.7 to 52.8 percent between 1966 and 1977; for Black males under 24, the percentage grew from 9.9 to 23.3 percent (Carnegie Council on Children, 1977). Although these figures are discouraging, evaluating costs and benefits is very helpful in recognizing that often decisions about having children have environmental and emotional aspects that are realistically perceived by adolescents.

CONCLUSION

Integrating useful factors from all the perspectives discussed might lead to a more complete understanding of Black adolescent pregnancy. When evaluating the initiation of sexual activity by adolescents, contraceptive use and childbearing can be considered behavioral outcomes of a decision-making process — an assessment of costs, benefits, and risks of alternative behaviors. The decision-making process can itself be analyzed with an eye toward interventive strategies that are aimed at encouraging more "beneficial" and less "costly" outcomes for individuals and for society.

Empirical evidence cited earlier clearly suggests that the costs of early childbearing are high, particularly in terms of interrupted schooling, and possibly frustrated future occupational attainment and income. Yet, as White (1979) suggests, the perception of "opportunity costs" among population subgroups may very likely vary with the actual distribution of opportunities. It is a truism that social, educational, and economic opportunities are not equally distributed among the population. Membership in a racial minority, residence in certain regions of the country or in inner-cities, being female, or starting poor in life all contribute to a real restriction of available opportunities. Black female adolescents from the inner-city have all these strikes against them, which serves as a partial explanation for their higher out-of-wedlock birthrates.

Schinke, Gilchrist, and Small (1979) provide such an analysis and a model for intervention. They note that the first step in the decision-making process is information gathering. At that point it is important that accurate information be available. This chapter has presented considerable evidence that teenagers are making decisions about sex and contraception with a great deal of erroneous information. Access to more reliable information from parents, schools, other professionals, or the mass media is often not forthcoming. The first step then is — as the access to knowledge theorist would argue — to promote efforts to get accurate information regarding the costs, benefits, and particularly the risks of teenage sex, contraception and childbearing to teenagers. Parents, in particular, as suggested, are under-used sources of such information.

The second critical step, according to Schinke, Gilchrist, and Small, is that accurate perception, comprehension and storage of the information occur. It is here that many psychological theorists predict trouble can happen. Whether due to unconscious needs, cognitive immaturity, or a shaky level of moral reasoning, some teenagers appear to resist or distort information about costs, benefits and risks. For the inner-city adolescent these "distortions" may not be distortions at all but may reflect good reality testing in that these youth do have limited opportunities when compared with suburban, middle-income adolescents. These accurate perceptions may in fact encourage rather than discourage adolescent sexual activity and childbearing.

Many of the crucial elements in an adolescent's decision-making remain relatively inaccessible to outside influence — or at least to the influence of policy-makers or service providers. Luker (1975) suggests that the costs of acknowledging intercourse and contraceptive use constitute one such example. The norms of the peer culture, which appear to figure highly in adolescent calculations of social costs and benefits, seem relatively impervious to overt influences from the outside. When adolescents evaluate their options, they are influenced by their expectations and aspirations for the future, as well as a complex interaction of influences from the more or less intimate social environment which includes ethnic, class, and sex role norms and values. These specific influences are difficult to identify, much less to manipulate.

The approaches presented in this chapter suggest a host of possible interventions aimed at decreasing the incidence of unprotected sex and childbearing among teenagers. We can direct policy and programs toward increasing the supply of accurate information regarding the costs, benefits and risks of unprotected intercourse and early childbearing. We can encourage communication about sex, contraception and childbearing between parents and children, among adolescent peers, and especially between adolescent partners. The media and the schools could play significant roles in this effort, although it seems clear that we cannot underestimate the potential role of parents.

We need to work with adolescents in helping them overcome barriers to understanding such information so they may translate it into terms that make such information clearly relevant to their own lives. Some of this training can go on in formal or informal teaching situations. Other teenagers may need special help to overcome psychological problems that "distort" their understanding of both the causes and consequences of their behaviors. Some teenagers may be too immature to handle this information and to make responsible choices. For those teenagers we need to be more sensitive as adults to this vulnerability and trust they will grow out of their immaturity relatively unscathed.

We can introduce alternatives to early childbearing, propose opportunities which are perceived by teens as more valuable and more certain than the risky benefits of unprotected sex. Clearly one way to foster perception of alternative opportunities is to ensure than information and contraception are in fact available, for they are not currently available to significant portions of the adolescent population. Further, if it is understood that poverty contributes to the problem of adolescent pregnancy, social policies must be simultaneously reoriented and programs restructured to address these macro-level needs. An improved service delivery system to all low-income adolescents that addresses prevention issues would do more to decrease the adolescent birthrate and other problems that affect this target group, while enhancing their life opportunities.

REFERENCES

Adler, A. (1956). Heinz L. & Rowena R. Ansbacker (Eds.), *Individual psychology of Alfred Adler: A systematic presentation in selection from his writings*. New York: W. W. Norton and Co.

Ajzen, I. & Fishbein, M. (1980). *Understanding attitudes and predicting social behavior*. Englewood Cliffs, NJ: Prentice-Hall.

Bauman, K. E. & Udry, J. R. (1972). Powerlessness and regularity of contraception in urban Negro male sample: A research note. *Journal of Marriage and the Family, 1*(34), 112-114.

Bernard, J. S. (1966). *Marriage and family among Negroes*. Englewood Cliffs, NJ: Prentice-Hall.

Berndt, T. (1979). Developmental changes in conformity to peers and parents. *Developmental Psychology, 6*(15), 608-616.

Blake, I. K. (1979). Early language use and the Black child: A speech act analysis of mother-child inputs and outputs. Paper presented at the Bi-Annual Meeting of the Society for Research in Child Development, San Francisco.

Brittain, C. (1963). Adolescent choices and parent-peer cross-pressures. *American Sociological Review, 3*(28), 385-391.

Broen, P. (1972). The verbal environment of the language-learning child. *American Speech and Hearing Association Monographs*, 17.

Card, J. & Wise, L. (1978). Teenage mothers and fathers: The impact of early childbearing on the parents' personal and professional lives. *Family Planning Perspectives, 10*, 199.

Chestang, L. (1980). Character development in a hostile environment. Reprinted in Martin Blood (Ed.), *Life Span Development*. New York: Macmillan Co.

Chilman, C. (1978). Adolescent sexuality in a changing American society. Washington, DC: U.S. Department of Health, Education and Welfare.

Clark, K. B. (1965). *Dark ghetto: Dilemmas of social power*. New York: Harper and Row.

Costanzo, P. & Shaw, M. (1966). Conformity as a function of age level. *Child Development, 4*, 967-977.

Craig, T. & Huffine, C. (1976). Correlates of patient attendance in an inner-city mental health clinic. *American Journal of Psychiatry, 1*(233), 61-64.

Cromwell, V. L. & Cromwell, R. E. (1978). Perceived dominance in decision-making and conflict resolution among Anglo, Black, and Chicano couples. *Journal of Marriage and the Family, 40*(6), 749-759.

Curtis, R. L. (1975). Adolescent orientations toward parents and peers: Variations by sex, age and socio-economic status. *Adolescence, 10*(40), 483-494.

Cvetkovich, G., Grote, B., Lieberman, E. & Miller, W. (1978). Sex role development and teenage fertility-related behavior. *Adolescence, 50*(13), 231-236.

Dulit, E. (1972). Adolescent thinking à la Piaget: The formal stage. *Journal of Youth and Adolescence, 4*(1), 281-301.

Edwards, L., Steinman, M., Arnold, K. & Hakanson, E. (1980). Adolescent pregnancy prevention services in high school clinics. *Family Planning Perspectives, 190*, 12(1), 6-14.

Elkind, D. (1967). Egocentrism in adolescence. *Child Development, 38*(4), 1025-34.

Elkind, D. (1975). Recent research on cognitive development in adolescence. In J. E. Dragastin and G. H. Elder, Jr. (Eds.), *Adolescence in the life cycle*. Washington, DC: Hemisphere.

Evans, J., Selstad, G. & Welcher, W. (1976). Fertility control behavior & attitudes before and after abortion, childbearing or negative pregnancy test. *Family Planning Perspectives, 8*(4), 192-200.

Fiester, A. R. & Rudestam, K. E. (1973). A multivariate analysis of the early dropout process. *Journal of Consulting and Conical Psychology, 1*(43), 100-109.

Finkel, M. & Finkel, D. (1975). Sexual and contraceptive knowledge, attitudes and behaviors of male adolescents. *Family Planning Perspectives, 7*(6), 256-260.

Fischman, S. H. & Palley, H. A. (1978). Adolescent unwed motherhood: Implications for a national family policy. *Health and Social Work 3*(1), 30-46.

Fox, G. (1979). The family's influence on adolescent sexual behaviors. *Children Today, 3*(8), 21-25.

Furie, S. (1966). Birth control and the lower-class unmarried mother. *Social Work, 11*(1), 42-49.

Furstenberg, F. (1976). *Unplanned parenthood: The social consequences of teenage childbearing*. New York: Free Press.

Garfield, S. (1971). Research on client variables in psychotherapy. In A. Bergin and S. Garfield (Eds.), *Handbook of psychotherapy and behavior change*. New York: John Wiley and Sons.

Giddings, P. (1984). *When and where I enter . . . The impact of Black women on race and sex in America*. New York: William Morrow and Company.

Goldfarb, J., Mumford, D. M., Schum, D. A., Smith, D. B., Flowers, G. & Schum, C. (1977). An attempt to detect "pregnancy susceptibility" in indigent adolescent girls. *Journal of Youth and Adolescents, 2*(6), 127-144.

Goldsmith, S., Gabrielson, M. & Gabrielson, I. (1972). Teenagers, sex, and contraception. *Family Planning Perspectives, 1*(4).

Greer, J. G. & Lesniak, M. A. (1979). Community linkages and outreach services in adolescent contraceptive clinic programs. *Public Health Reports, 94,* 5, 415-419.

Hammond, J. & Enoch, J. R. (1976). Conjugal power relations among Black working class families. *Journal of Black Studies, 7*(1), 107-127.

Hendricks, L. (1982). Unmarried Black adolescent fathers' attitudes toward abortion, contraception, and sexuality: A preliminary report. *Society for Adolescent Medicine, 2,* 199-203.

Hogan, D. P. & Kitagawa, E. M. (1983). Family factors in the fertility of Black adolescents. Unpublished manuscript. Chicago: Population Research Center, University of Chicago.

Holt, G. S. (1972). The ethno-linguistic approach to speech-language learning. In Arthur L. Smith (Ed.), *Language, communication and rhetoric in Black America.* New York: Harper and Row.

Hyman, H. H. & Reed, J. S. (1969). Black matriarchy reconsidered: Evidence from secondary analysis of sample surveys. *Public Opinion Quarterly, 33*(3), 346-354.

Jekel, J. F., Harrison, J. T., Bancroft, D. R., Tyler, N. C. & Klerman, L. V. (1975). A comparison of the health index and subsequent babies born to school-age mothers. *American Journal of Public Health, 65*(4), 370-374.

Jessor, S. & Jessor, R. (1975). Transition from virginity to nonvirginity among youth: A social-psychological study over time. *Developmental Psychology, 4*(11), 473-484.

Johnson, L. B. & Staples, R. E. (1976). Family planning and the young minority male: A pilot project. *Family Coordinator, 28*(4), 535-543.

Kanter, J. & Zelnik, M. (1974). Sexual experience of young unmarried women in the U.S. *Family Planning Perspectives, 4*(6), 74-80.

Kaplan, H., Smith, P. & Pokorny, A. (1979). Psychosocial antecedents of unwed motherhood among indigent adolescents. *Journal of Youth and Adolescents, 8*(2), 181-207.

Keefe, D. E. (1983). Governor Reagan, welfare reform, and AFDC fertility. *Social Service Review, 2*(57), 234-253.

Koenig, M. A. & Zelnik, M. (1982). Repeat pregnancies among metropolitan area teenagers: 1971-1979. *Family Planning Perspectives, 14*(5), 239-247.

Ladner, J. (1972). *Tomorrow's tomorrow: The Black woman.* New York: Doubleday and Company, Inc.

Lee, S. & Temerlin, M. (1970). Social class, diagnosis and prognosis for psychotherapy. *Psychotherapy: Theory, Research, Practice, 7*(3), 181-185.

Luker, K. (1975). *Taking chances: Abortion and decision not to contracept.* Berkeley, California: University of California Press.

MacDonald, A. (1970). Internal-external locus of control and the practice of birth control. *Psychological Reports, 27*(1), 206.

Mead, G. H. (1934). *Self and Society.* Chicago: University of Chicago Press.

Miller, W. (1976, September). Sexual and contraceptive behavior in young unmarried women. *Primary Care.*

Moore, K. A. & Cardwell, S. B. (1976). Out-of-wedlock pregnancy and childbearing. Washington, DC: Urban Institute.

Mott, F. L. & Maxwell, N. L. (1981). School-age mothers: 1968 and 1979. *Family Planning Perspectives, 13*(6), 287-292.

National Center for Health Statistics (1978, 1981). *Advance report: Final natality statistics,* Supplement to *Monthly Vital Statistics Report.* Hyattsville, MD: U.S. Department of Health, Education and Welfare.

Neimark, E. (1975). Intellectual development during adolescence. In F. Horowitz (Ed.) Reviews of child development research (Vol. 4). Chicago: University of Chicago Press.

Pannor, R. (1971). *The unmarried father.* New York: Springer.

Piaget, J. (1952). *The origins of intelligence in children.* New York: W. W. Norton and Company, Inc.

Powell, G. J. & Fuller, M. (1972). The variables for positive self-concept among young Black Southern adolescents. *Journal of the National Medical Association, 64*, 522-526.

Rains, P. (1971). *Becoming an unwed mother*. Chicago: Aldine.

Rainwater, L. (1966). Crucible of identity: The new lower class family. *Daedalus, 95*(1), 1976-216.

Reichelt, P. & Werley, H. (1975). Contraception, abortion, and VD: Teenager's knowledge and the effect of education. *Family Planning Perspectives, 7*(2), 83-88.

Rosenberg, M. (1979). *Conceiving the self*. New York: Basic Books.

Rosenberg, M. & Simmons, R. (1972). *Black and White self-esteem: The urban school child*. Washington, DC: The American Sociological Association.

Rovinsky, J. (1972). Abortion recidivism: A problem in preventive medicine. *Obstetrics and Gynecology, 39*(5), 649-659.

Rubin, L. (1976). *Worlds of pain*. New York: Basic Books.

Schinke, S., Gilchrist, L. & Small, R. (1978). Preventing unwanted adolescent pregnancy: A cognitive-behavioral approach. *American Journal of Orthopsychiatry, 1*(49), 81-88.

Schofield, M. G. (1965). *The sexual behavior of young people*. Boston: Little, Brown and Company.

Shaw, F., Zelnik, M. & Kantner, J. (1975). Unprotected intercourse among unwed teenagers. *Family Planning Perspectives, 7*(2), 39-44.

Shearer, J. B. & Shearer, S. B. (1979). *Contraception and common sense: Conventional methods reconsidered*. New York: Population Council.

Solomon, B. (1976). *Black empowerment*. New York: Columbia University Press.

Stack, C. (1974). *All our kin: Strategies for survival in a Black community*. New York: Harper & Row, Inc.

Tenhouten, W. D. (1970). The Black family: Myth and reality. *Psychiatry, 33*(2), 145-173.

Testa, M. (1983). Interim report from the 1982 adolescent parent outreach survey. Unpublished manuscript. National Opinion Research Center, Chicago.

Thompson, K. (1980). A comparison of Black and White adolescents beliefs about having children. *Journal of Marriage and the Family, 1*(42), 133.

Thompson, L. & Spanier, G. (1978). Influence of parents, peers and partners on the contraceptive use of college men and women. *Journal of Marriage and the Family, 3*(40), 481-492.

U.S. Bureau of Census (1980). Families Maintained by Female households, 1970-1979. *Current Population Reports*, Series P-23, No. 107. Washington, DC: Government Printing Office.

Vincent, C. (1961). *Unmarried mothers*. New York: Free Press.

White, L. (1979). The correlates of urban fertility in the U.S. 1960-1970. *Journal of Marriage and the Family, 4*(41), 715-726.

Wilson, W. S. (1984). The Black underclass. *Wilson Quarterly*, 88-99.

Wilson, W. S. & Aponte, R. (Forthcoming.) Urban poverty. *Annual Review of Sociology*, 11.

Yankelovich, D. (1969). *Generations apart*. New York: CBS.

Yette, S. F. (1971). *The choice: The issue of survival in America*. New York: Putnam.

Zelnik, M. & Kantner, J. (1977). Sexual and contraceptive experience of young unmarried women in the United States, 1976 and 1971. *Family Planning Perspectives, 9*(2), 55-71.

Zelnik, M. & Kantner, J. (1980). Sexual activity, contraceptive use and pregnancy among metropolitan-area teenagers: 1971-1979. *Family Planning Perspectives, 12*(5), 230-237.

Zongker, C. E. (1977). The self-concept of pregnant adolescent girls. *Adolescence, 12*(48), 477-488.

"How Would You Feel . . . ?": Clinical Interviews With Black Adolescent Mothers

Nancy A. Boxill

ABSTRACT. This chapter explores the experiences of twelve poor Black adolescent mothers as related through clinical interviews. In these interviews, the young women described their growing years, decision-making processes, experiences of parenting, and feelings about the life-altering challenges they faced. Data from the interviews produced four themes: the perceived failure of their own parents and family life; the lack of satisfactory intimate relationships with peers and others; the experience of being simultaneously too young and too old; and the challenge of becoming a good mother. The collective descriptions of their experiences are then reviewed in a current social and economic context.

The uncomfortably high rate of births to adolescents has claimed the attention and concern of nearly all Americans. Awareness of this problem—whether through the media, professional or popular literature, or personal experience—has sparked dialogue, confusion, and calls to action. Informed dialogue, when not merely a lament, is positive, for through informed dialogue we go beyond ourselves to attend in a serious and focused manner to the multifaceted experience of Black adolescent parents. Through this important process we may come to know and understand the adolescents, ourselves, and our society as reflected in our youth.

The information gleaned from a variety of sources calls us to action. We plan and implement health care, educational, day care, and employment and training programs as solutions to a perhaps

Nancy A. Boxill, PhD, is Associate Professor and Chair of the Child and Family Services Department at The Atlanta University School of Social Work. Dr. Boxill is a child psychologist. She serves as a consultant to several state agencies and is in private practice. Her research, teaching, and practice focus on minority children and youth with special interest in child psychology, child development, and parent/child relationships.

poorly defined problem troubling a mystifying target population. This chapter does not provide a discussion of causes or suggest solutions to this circumstance. Rather it describes the experiences of a group of Black adolescent mothers as reported during clinical interviews. From the data of individual experience flows understanding, enlightened dialogue, and points of entry for both clinical practice and program planning.

The Black adolescent female who elects, is forced, or by default becomes a parent has achieved virtually the same levels of cognitive, affective, physiological and social development as her White counterpart. The quagmires and challenges of adolescence are dramatic and tumultuous for both Black and White adolescents. Stresses, strengths and struggles arise in each experience. Black adolescent parents, however, live with the unique circumstances of racism and oppression which are woven into the context of their experiences. During an already stressful time, the Black adolescent mother must negotiate the limitations and unpleasant realities which racism, oppression and poverty place on her choices. In the midst of trying to develop and express their own identities and plans for the future; discovering and managing physiological and psychological changes; attaining comfort with their skills and abilities; and enjoying the fun of teenage years, this group must face and survive the deliberate constraints of individual potential that accompany racism and its ensuing oppression.

This combination of ordinary and specific stresses is the subject of this chapter. The title is taken directly from an interview in which an adolescent mother whose experience is reported here, pointedly asked "How would you feel if you were a poor Black teenager with no education, not job, and a child to support on your own?" From this provocative question, it was clear she had internalized societal attitudes. She experienced those attitudes as an impediment to an economically and perhaps emotionally stable existence. That single question prompted exploration of the feelings and experiences of a group of poor Black adolescent mothers with whom I work as a mental health professional.

DESCRIPTION OF THE POPULATION AND PROCESS

Over the course of eight months, individual clinical interviews were conducted with twelve Black adolescent mothers, 16 to 19 years old. Each was poor and receiving some type of income support, i.e., AFDC, child care, parental assistance or other allotments. All had a history of limited educational achievement. Four were employed part-time. Three had continuing relationships with their child's father. All were enrolled in educational or vocational programs. Each girl was interviewed at least seven times for approximately 45 minutes. They described their growing years, decision-making processes, experiences of parenting in difficult circumstances, as well as feelings and beliefs about their future.

The material in this chapter was thematized in the mode of phenomenological investigation as described by Coliazzi (1973), Giorgi (1970), and Wertz (1982) to permit shared experiences to be grouped for enhanced understanding. This approach can benefit clinicians, program planners, and others working with similar populations. Within the descriptive material, four themes emerged:

1. Perceived failures of their own parents
2. Lack of satisfactory intimate relations with peers and others
3. Experience of being simultaneously too young and too old
4. The challenge of becoming a good mother

The use of quotation marks following indicates actual language used by the adolescents.

THEME 1:
PERCEIVED FAILURES OF THEIR OWN PARENTS

Few interviews with any of the adolescents were without some discussion of family relationships. While the specifics of each family were of course different — i.e., family size, birth order, relationship to siblings, etc. — each teenage mother described experiences of being "let down" by her parents. Each in their own terms described not getting along with one or both parents. Constant fighting or bickering over small and/or large issues from "nothing" to undone chores, curfews, school attendance and performance were frequent elements of discussion. More important to the girls than the focus of the argument was the distinction that most of their years at home were spent fighting or avoiding their parents.

Often their descriptions of family life included examples of parents and children not being able to understand each other. The adolescents described a series of experiences which they named "living in the wrong house," "speaking another language," or "living in a different time or place." Most described continually "trying to get through" to their parents, and experiencing their parents as being inaccessible. Many eventually "just stopped trying" to make the connection. Comments such as "she should have known," "he could have done more," "she never said anything," "how can you talk to someone like that?" frequently punctuated a recounting of their desire to be understood. Several interviewees described long-standing feelings of not being cared for. Poignant descriptions of being lonely and wanting desperately to find "someone who will really care" generally ended with hopeless phrases such as "but I don't think I will" or "not likely." There was usually anger as well as frustration as they described "having to do it on my own."

Nevertheless, most of the young mothers interviewed expressed "really" loving their mothers and/or fathers. All of them perceived their parents to be uninformed and powerless to make changes in their own lives or in the life of the family unit. This perception was confirmed for the adolescent when she approached the parent with feelings of being caught, confused, troubled, or in need of information, skill, advocacy or money only to find the parent impotent. Repeated perceived lack of successful action by the parent, confirmed the child's view. Although some expressed the belief that their parent was doing the best he or she could, they were often disappointed in the results or consequences of parental action.

On face value it may appear there is no new information contained in the preceding discussion. Indeed, much of it sounds as though these experiences could have been reported by any adolescent in America. Drawing this conclusion, however, ignores an important, albeit insidious, effect of racism, oppression and poverty. The combination of feeling out of place, not understood, and not cared for may seem generic to adolescence. It becomes quite population-specific, however, when the concept of perceived powerlessness is superimposed. The intention of racism, poverty, and oppression is to ensure that a group feels and believes itself not to be in control of its own destiny. In fact, none of these parents were financially, educationally, or politically able to make real or immediate changes in their own lives or the lives of their families. The vital importance of the experience reported in this theme is that today there are Black adolescents who believe their parents — whose role it is to teach them about the world and guide them to adulthood — are ineffective.

The perception of the adolescents was that their parents had serious personal faults. None wished to emulate those parental behaviors. There is perhaps no greater indictment of racism than its effect of fostering a belief system in youth which includes a lack of confidence in parents and other adults who are seen as unable to manage the world successfully. Racism affected the belief system of these Black adolescents further by encouraging a sense that their parents were by default unable to create and shape their own futures.

THEME 2:
LACK OF SATISFACTORY RELATIONSHIPS
WITH PEERS AND OTHERS

The majority of the subjects repeatedly expressed a desire to steer clear of "close relationships." They described how they deliberately structured their behavior to avoid opportunities for lasting relationships. Comments such as, "it's not good to get close to too many people," "I used to have best friends but not anymore," "I just think it's better to stay alone," were frequent. In exploring these and similar remarks, the girls more clearly discussed their apprehensions about "trusting" another person. They were earnestly concerned about having relationships in which the other person was always taking, and they were always giving. Previous close relationships had been unhappy and fallen far short of their expectations, including in many instances the relationship with their child's father. At this juncture in their lives most of the girls were not willing to take such a risk again. They described behaving in an almost mechanical fashion toward others, performing only superficial actions, just enough to have a person to "talk to on the phone" or a buddy for "hanging out." These feelings and behaviors applied to males as well as females.

For the overwhelming majority of the girls their first as well as ensuing sexual experiences had been void of physical pleasure. Most reported engaging in sexual intercourse as a means of experiencing temporary closeness which they had hoped would lead to meaningful and lasting relationships. Here again they were givers not receivers of that which they sought. The pregnancies that resulted from the sexual encounters were not experienced as a blending of two persons, rather as a fact or consequence of their actions. The birth of their children in most cases was not experienced as the result of loving. For the adolescent mother merely the recounting of these events and how they turned out was itself an emotionally unpleasant, even sour, experience.

Similarly, relationships with adults were experienced as punitive, confusing, and often insincere. Predictably perhaps many girls questioned the motives and genuineness of the human service providers whose task it was to assist in meeting their needs. Such comments as "I know she doesn't like me," "she must have never been young," "what's wrong with her?", "it's not her child or her life," indicated a good deal of hostility and distance between the Black adolescent and those adults who had been paid to help. Thus the adolescent parent once again felt rejected and/or alone, without adult guidance or assistance.

In sad and dispassionate tones many described not even looking for real connections with others, not even with peers. They expressed a willingness to accept fluid, superficial, and self-serving interactions with peers. Only on rare occasions did any of the young women admit such behavior was indeed not their preferred course of action, only a safe mask from which they could see others without being seen.

The content of this theme may bode ill for the immediate future of Black families. If these Black adolescent parents continue to be without meaningful, successful relationships with others, we may well be moving toward a community of persons who cannot, or will not trust and cooperate with each other. The logging of a series of unsuccessful interpersonal relationships at such an early age does not enable the adolescent parent to begin the process of teaching trusting interpersonal relationship skills to their children. While mother-child bonding may well occur, its usefulness as a base for moving into the larger world may be weakened.

Of particular interest is the absence of a solid or continuing relationship with the child's father. Although a marriage may not be the optimal solution in each case, it is often helpful for some level of relationship to be continued. The current state of relationships between Black adolescent parents may be a signal that the role of adolescent father is currently too ambiguous, leaving both parents unable to know just what to embrace (McGuire, 1983). This role ambiguity presents a challenge to build a community of adults who can and do care for their children. Without such an effort, there is a danger of bringing truth to the prediction that by the year 2000, our communities will be populated by the so-called "permanent underclass" of mothers who are the sole support of their children (U.S. Commission on Civil Rights, 1983). This is clearly a subject for dialogue and action.

THEME 3:
BEING SIMULTANEOUSLY
TOO YOUNG AND TOO OLD

Discussions about the future invariably evoked ambivalence about the adolescents' ability to succeed in a chosen path or goal. Many described themselves as being too young and too old in the same breath.

In effect they experienced a twilight of transition. Adolescence is traditionally viewed as a period of transition. The term "twilight of transition" embraces the traditional concept while enhancing the meaning to indicate an impending and forced close of such a period. The economic, educational, and political realities of these adolescents do not permit a languid or natural closing of a most difficult phase of the life cycle. The poor Black adolescent often must quickly, if erroneously, move toward adulthood with insufficient preparation and adult support.

The sense of being caught in an impending current which thrusts them into adulthood was evidenced by the following comments:

> I am too young to have to make all these decisions. I am too old to have to ask for advice. I should be able to figure things out on my own. I am too young to have to be in control of everything. I am too old to have to depend on my parents. I am too young to get a job. I am too old to take hand-outs. I am too young to be treated as a child. I am too young to have to be grown-up. I am too old to do childish things. I am too young to know the answers. I am too old to be so confused. I am too young to be a mother. I am too old to be told what to do.

These quotations have deliberately not been placed in dichotomous lists, as they were expressed more as whirlwinds of feelings, not distinct choices. With few variations, the sense of "suspension" is clearly revealed. Many of the mothers felt trapped and out of control of their interactions, even with their children.

The resolution of this twilight of transition is critical to the survival of the Black community. Our young adults in transition stand without personal financial resources and frequently without a network of persons able to provide financial assistance. The poor Black adolescent parent is forced to rely on hand-outs, welfare, loans, and an inconsistent share of the most minimal resources. This adolescent then resorts to making short-range and unsatisfactory decisions, i.e., moving into overcrowded quarters with a friend, taking a job without having secured viable child care, etc. The combination of racism, poverty and limited educational achievement quickly defeats the most energetic and ardent Black adolescent parent desiring to challenge her lot. Far too often her frustration is swallowed in exchange for food stamps. Her anger smolders slowly, even toward the human service providers whose assistance is a further reminder of her feelings of inadequacy.

THEME 4:
THE CHALLENGE OF BECOMING
A "GOOD MOTHER"

The only goal-oriented theme to emerge was that of experiencing oneself as a "good mother." The adolescents' definitions shared some commonalities: For most, "good" meant being caring, alert to the child's needs, loving, a firm disciplinarian, a good provider, making the child look attractive, and living in a nice place. Most often the adolescent mothers talked about their own goals for parenting as the antithesis of the parenting they recalled experiencing.

All but three clearly expressed a desire not to use their own mothers as role models for what lay ahead. Although every adolescent repeatedly expressed love for her own mother, to a person they wanted to "do it better."

Their excitement about the challenge of parenting was evident from their facial expressions and animated conversations about parenting. Many shared enthusiastic, unsolicited examples of their child's successes or new acquisitions in learning in which as mothers they had been instrumental.

> I taught her how to eat with a fork last week. It took almost two days, but we just worked at it. Sometimes she tried to use her fingers to eat, but mostly I just kept telling her "very good," and "one more time." She's really funny, you know, but she sure is smart.

When the discussion shifted toward the severe reality of parenting in difficult circumstances, their aloneness was visible and spoken. These discussions typically evoked a soft sadness. It seemed to be easy to want to be different, yet difficult to know how to go about being different. Most often the young mothers were distressed when confronted with the level and quality of care their children required. The brutal realization that babies require care twenty-four hours a day, seven days a week was not in line with their own adolescent, carefree and unscheduled life style. The full weight of discovering that children are not always cute, happy, or playful but may present many inconveniences was frustrating and maddening. Periodically many of the adolescent mothers simply neglected to attend to the necessary mothering tasks. In fact, this is easily understood as the habitual, widely fluctuating pattern of adolescent behavior. Their intent was to gain temporary relief, and return to being a child having fun. The intent was never pointedly to neglect their children. On the contrary, the spirit and will to be "good mothers" loomed large. The fear of falling short was with them everyday. "I don't know how now . . . but someday I will," typifies the cautious, resigned enthusiasm they frequently displayed.

Consequently, all were grateful for any emotional support they received from their peers, and described a series of relationships which were circumscribed around mothering. In a very concrete way, these adolescent mothers drew together to form informal emotional support networks. Without financial or other tangible resources, the mothers served as cheerleaders for each other. The network offered an arena for working out new patterns of parental interaction.

CONCLUSION

The descriptive material thematized in this chapter is not purported to be necessarily representative in experience or behavior of all poor Black adolescent female parents. Rather we are made privy to personal and general expressions of a sample of that population. The content of the themes can and does make explicit that which is often known or believed on an implicit level.

Material from the interviews described highlights several issues which are worthy of discussion and which call for action. Too often the most skillful and well-intentioned practitioners throw up their hands in either truncated success or expensive failure. Their frustration is frequently accompanied by laments of not understanding. It may well be the extent to which our own adolescent experience differs from that of today's poor Black adolescent, does prevent us from understanding. The Black adolescent mothers who participated in these interviews have provided us with a glimpse into the general experience. Understanding of individual experience enables us to demystify the group and their experience.

Secondly, service providers are often faced with Black adolescent parents who are difficult to reach and/or serve effectively. This circumstance may occur because the adolescent mother is feeling too young, too old, too isolated, too overwhelmed, too angry, too sad to do more than is minimally necessary to receive the tangible benefits of the service. The special sharing in which these girls participated can assist frustrated clinicians in arriving at an entry point for promoting change. It may also provide assistance in understanding and working with an otherwise recalcitrant or seemingly uncooperative adolescent mother who needs help. Practitioners who regularly work with adolescents are acutely aware of the need to establish a relationship quickly with the client. Most teens don't give you a second chance. The themes which emerged in these interviews make it possible to discover alternative points of entry for clinicians. Utilization of such information may move the clinician more quickly toward a genuine helping and helpful relationship.

Third, the issues and material discussed here provide excellent qualitative information for those charged with program planning and implementation for Black adolescent mothers and their children. Careful review and testing of the generalizations presented in the chapter may assist in the development of new programs which are less ambiguous in their moral message and more effective in their attempts to redirect sexual attitudes and behaviors in adolescents. The discussion of new, clear and effective roles, and functions of adolescent fathers is necessary and timely. This void in childrearing presents an entry point for program planners, as does sometimes devoting serious attention to neighborhoods where Black teens face economic and other struggles beyond the normative struggles of adolescence.

Finally, thoughtful reflection upon the themes which emerged in these interviews challenges us again to focus on combatting the negative effects of racism, poverty, sexism, and oppression. If it is too late to escape the predicted wave of a permanent underclass of mi-

nority women and their children by the year 2000, it is not too late
to forestall the erosion of the strengths of Black families. Our ability
to understand the experience of another person or group of persons
portends our capacity to try to meet their needs effectively. If this is
not the seminal issue, it is at least a contribution to the dialogue.

REFERENCES

Bode, J. (1980). *Kids having kids: The unwed teenage parent.* New York: Franklin Watts
Publisher.
Coliazzi, P. (1973). *Reflections and research in psychology.* Iowa: Kendall-Hunt Publishing
Co.
Disadvantage women and their children: A growing crisis. (1983). Washington, DC: U.S.
Commission on Civil Rights.
Giorgi, A. (1970). *Psychology as a human science.* New York: Harper and Row.
Lindsay, J. W. (1981). *Teen pregnancy.* Buena Park, CA: Morning Glory Press.
McGee, E. A. (1982). *Too little, too late: Services for teenage parents.* New York: Ford
Foundation.
McGuire, P. (1983). *It won't happen to me.* New York: Dell Publisher.
Wertz, F. J. (1982). Procedures in phenomenal research and the question of validity. *Studies in
the Social Sciences,* Carrollton, GA: West Georgia College, *XXIII*, 29-47.

Consumer Perceptions of Black Adolescent Mothers

Alva P. Barnett

ABSTRACT. This paper reports data from interviews with Black adolescent mothers who receive a cross-section of health and social services. This study identified factors related to the utilization of services by adolescent mothers; it described how they perceived the identified problems, what their needs are as mothers and their view of services they receive. Implications and suggestions for program development processes are outlined, with an emphasis on the importance of the adolescent mothers' potential contributions to program planning development, as well as to their own social development. Comprehensive services will strengthen those aspects of social development that Black adolescent mothers themselves recognize as significant as well, it is hoped, open new vistas for teens in our society.

The extent to which consumers utilize services, in part, is due to their perceptions of their problems and needs, as well as the services they receive. This study of Black adolescent mothers is concerned with how these mothers perceive the meaning of their interactions with a cross-section of health and social services. The focus on consumer perceptions suggests areas in which practitioners, and other scientific and professional experts, should concentrate their attention to improve the effectiveness of service delivery and increase consumer utilization. Also the perceptions of transactions between the consumers and service provider representatives are related to the extent of consumer utilization (Bice & White, 1971).

The social development of adolescent mothers needs our utmost attention and support, especially when we consider adolescent

Alva P. Barnett, MSW, MPH, PhD, is Assistant Professor in the School of Social Work at the University of Nebraska at Omaha. Present research and scholarly interests include adolescent health and development, the Black family, adolescent parenting, and international health care. Dr. Barnett's previous work experience includes over 12 years in clinical social work and the mental health field.

mothers are among those in the next generation likely to assume many decision-making roles and responsibilities (Bilsborrow, 1977; Schwartz, 1981). Adolescent mothers deserve understanding, not just to explore health and social expenditures, but to explore the context of their creative and substantive contributions to the welfare of the nation. Furthermore, these adolescents are immediately responsible for the training, early social skills development, and guidance of subsequent adult generations. Aside from concern with future generations, emphasizing the social development of adolescent mothers warrants more thought, understanding, and action on the part of all professional disciplines.

The following facts should be considered:

1. the increasing number of births to adolescents who are choosing childrearing;
2. the health, economic, and social consequences associated with adolescent parenting;
3. the national costs of providing medical and social services to the adolescent mother and her infant;
4. the underutilization of the limited services by adolescent mothers; and
5. the virtual lack of participation by these consumers in program planning and development efforts, so increased utilization, program coordination, and greater effectiveness may result.

The recognition of the need for consumer participation, is based partly on the assumption that "planning must reflect the problems, values, and/or needs in the different segments of the total social system . . . a continuous process in the machinery for social development" (Pandey, 1981). Furthermore, Massey (1980) states that "the better we promote the concept of mutual benefit resulting from the consumer-provider partnership the better will be the . . . care available for all." This partnership must begin by providers acknowledging and understanding the adolescent mothers and *their* perceptions of problems, needs, and services.

RATIONALE

A brief overview of related facts and figures, consequences, and interdisciplinary discourse persistently associated with adolescent motherhood will, it is hoped, reveal the rationale for this chapter.

Within the last decade and a half, the population of adolescent mothers has been increasing (Furstenberg, 1976; Guttmacher Institute, 1976; Bayh, 1976; Card & Wise, 1978). Also an increasing percentage of pregnant adolescents are single and keeping their babies. More recently, more births are occurring to younger adolescent mothers, ages 13-14, even 12 years of age (Bogue, 1977; National Center for Health Statistics, 1978; Guttmacher, 1981). This decrease in the age of these mothers is happening while total birth rates have been decreasing (Reinhold, 1977).

Another serious concern of adolescent motherhood is its frequent, less than positive social, economic, and health consequences (Bolton, 1980). These might include:

1. foreshortened educational training for job competencies, that is, minimal or inadequate preparation for the competitive job market, and frequently the inability to maintain other self-sufficient responsibilities assumed in the adult role such as employment (Trussel, 1976; Ogg, 1976);
2. difficulty in finding adequate child care provisions, despite the initial Congressional support of comprehensive legislation for quality day care services; and
3. limited time and flexibility to interact with peer groups (De-Lissovoy, 1973) which often increases feelings of isolation and a sense of hopelessness.

Self-development and the supportive enhancement of social skills can be severely compromised. In addition, feelings of isolation and hopelessness are likely to increase associated risk factors of the infants, for instance, child abuse and neglect.

Therefore, early motherhood can be considered an event that is likely to impede the acquisition of social skills and development of self-sufficiency; in social work, we refer to this dilemma as self-determination. This event demands new social skills even before the adolescent mother has negotiated many of the roles and tasks of adolescence (Bruce, 1978).

Adolescent motherhood is an issue that might well be considered within the human development strategy for social development. Aspects of this strategy focus on productive capacity, participatory skills, and cultural experiences which are likely to enhance the capacities and opportunities of the present generation without diminishing the potential for future generations (Pandey, 1981).

In relationship to adolescent mothers, social development needs to involve a commitment to equitable participation and respect for individual lifestyles and cultural values, thus allowing optimal utilization of all human resources. In regard to enhancing human capacity and opportunities, other features of human development strategy deserve attention. The quality and quantity of social services, and their accessibility and accountability, are closely related to "the stage of national development, social priorities . . . political commitment . . ." (Guttmacher, 1981). Garbarino (1981) supports this view when he states that "the utilization and dissemination of research-based knowledge, concerning children and youth, has very low priority in the activities of social scientists, policy makers, and practitioners."

Human development strategies for our children have been ignored as we see when we examine the plethora of literature and research generated over a decade and a half. Services have increased—for instance, services have grown from 250 prior to 1970 to over 1,000 in 1977 (Forbush, 1981)—but have been considered inadequate to meet the multiple needs of the adolescent population.

Despite varied attempts to assist adolescent mothers, services can be seen to be underutilized in terms of consumer satisfaction of needs (Bureau of Community Health Services, 1978; Consumer Health Perspective, 1980). There are numerous reasons for this underutilization. For example, studies have shown that programs and services to adolescent mothers are piecemeal and not well coordinated; there is competition and little cooperation between programs; and most are developed by providers with little consumer input. The program planning and development process is largely generated by the agencies and/or their funding sources (Forbush & Leigh, 1977; National Association of Social Workers, 1982).

Social development strategies involve working toward improvement in the quality of both individual life and the level of living. This improvement is expected to result from appropriate responses and intervention to social as well as institutional changes in our society. Paiva (1981) has suggested a number of prerequisites for improving social services, two which are related to this study: (1) Participation should involve an ongoing partnership between consumers and providers of services (practitioners and other professionals); (2) Decision making should involve consumers and providers as they focus on the structure and modus operandi of service delivery.

Even with the attention that has been given adolescent mothers, very little is known regarding what the adolescent mother thinks, what she sees as her needs, and what meanings she attributes to her transactions with a cross-section of health and social services, and with the providers of these services. Fox (1974) states that "the success of a program in promoting well-being must be reflected in the life experience of its members." Thus the mere availability of intervention strategies is not sufficient to respond to the variation of adolescent mothers' life experiences and their perceived needs. It is essential to comprehend the individual adolescent and her perceptions, along several dimensions. Hence, this chapter hopes to identify and describe what the thoughts and feelings are of adolescent mothers as they consider their problems, needs, and the services they receive.

RESEARCH QUESTIONS

The following research questions were addressed in this study:

1. What are the selected demographic characteristics of the sample population of adolescent mothers interviewed?
2. What are the perceptions of their problems, according to the adolescent mothers? How are the identified problems described?
3. What services are needed by adolescent mothers as they perceive them, as consumers? What needs do services emphasize? What is the extent of need satisfaction?
4. What is the perception of services provided to and utilized by the adolescent mothers? Are service providers responsive to consumers' felt needs? How are the services that are emphasized evaluated?

METHOD

An interview schedule was developed and pretested with a series of structured questions. The participants in this study were 20 Black adolescent mothers who were active in a multiservice childcare program in a large inner-city alternative school. The sample for this exploratory-descriptive study represented 40 percent of the program's participants who were ages 13-18 at the time of their first birth.

Services within the childcare program are provided by caregivers and include: childcare while mothers are in class, parenting skills to mothers, and family intervention when necessary. Each young mother is assigned to a caregiver for the duration of her participation in the program. This childcare program is based in an alternative educational and medical facility where other support services are coordinated.

The sampling frame consisted of those adolescent mothers on the childcare program roster, and the sample population chosen was based on the availability of subjects. The homogeneity of the population was to provide better chances for valid and reliable data. However, generalizability to all Black adolescent mothers in our society is limited because of the selected survey population. Yet in choosing the sample subjects in this manner, relatively high representativeness of the survey population seemed to be achieved. This view is supported by Stouffer (1962) who stated that "if we had been able to interview all of the individuals . . . the result would differ from those in the sample by only a relatively small chance of error . . . ; in addition, small samples are useful in exploratory studies."

All 20 adolescent mothers asked to participate in this study agreed to the confidentiality that was maintained. The interviews were carried out in a private room within the agency and lasted an average of 45 minutes.

The questions were both close- and open-ended to yield factual and descriptive data. The information sought from each adolescent mother included the following: demographic information; specification and description of problems and the extent of these problems; identification of needs; and the identification and description of the types of services, quality of services, and extent of services utilized. Another segment of the interview focused on the extent and quality of support systems within the adolescent mother's life.

The functions of this investigation were to: (1) systematically portray the characteristics of a selected target population, and (2) determine the frequency and extent of distribution of certain variables. In addition, the qualitative aspects of this study were intended to facilitate an understanding of the target population, their perceptions, and their assigned meanings of transactions with the service providers.

FINDINGS

Major findings of this study are summarized on the basis of the four research questions previously stated:

1. Selected Demographic Data

The ethnic background of the selected population are Black Americans. One-half of the adolescent mothers were 17 years of age at the time of the interview. However, 16.5 years was the mean age of respondents at the time of their first birth. Two of the adolescent mothers had second births, representing 10 percent of the respondents; they were 15 and 16 years of age at the time of their first birth.

It was noted that 45 percent of the respondents, who were program participants when interviewed, were 17 years of age at the time of their first birth. This data suggests that many of these mothers continued comprehensive service utilization shortly after giving birth. One might surmise that parenting and child care support services increase the likelihood of this relatively high level of continued participation.

The grade levels completed by the mothers ranged from ninth to eleventh grades. The majority (60 percent) of the consumer respondents were twelfth-grade students who were near graduation at the time of the interview. A majority (55 percent) of the respondents had aspirations to continue their education beyond high school; they felt that the chances of reaching their educational goals were very good.

This selected demographic information suggests the mothers were able to continue their participation with services because of the design of the educational child care parenting program.

Family Configurations and Relationships

The majority of respondents were in the first generation of single mothers in their families; 75 percent of the respondents indicated that no members of their family of origin had been single adolescent parents.

The majority (60 percent) of the adolescent mothers who participated in this study lived with at least one parent, while 20 percent of this majority lived with both parents and siblings. Only one respondent lived with the father of her child and another lived alone with her child. The remaining respondents lived with other relatives. These findings indicate a relatively stable population, living within their family of origin.

The majority (65 percent) of the consumer respondents were either completely or moderately satisfied with their living situation.

Some were not satisfied with their situation; 35 percent desired to live alone with their children. However, they realized the impracticality of immediately satisfying the desire to live independently from their families.

2. Perception of Problems by Consumers

Some important trends were noted in the section which examined perception of problems. This section included questions regarding whether identified problem circumstances had improved, and who was most helpful to them with these problems.

In order to present a clear picture of the extent of the respondents' identified problems, their comments need to be included with the most important problems relating to adolescent motherhood as identified by consumer respondents:

1. A change occurred in their priorities which gave them less free time. "I can't go out any time I want to. So, I often take him with me." "I can't get out as often as I once did or without making plans ahead of time." "I don't go out as much as I used to. I just decided that I had to give something up. There is no major problem because it's just not top priority."
2. They had increased responsibility. "It is difficult in the morning having to dress the baby and myself, then try and get ready for school." "Since my second child, I have not been able to get enough rest. I must attend to both their needs and the first child is becoming very active." "Tending to my baby's needs is very time consuming—a big responsibility."
3. Conflict developed around their being independent of and dependent on their families, usually their mothers. "I can't talk to my mother. Now that I have a son, my mother doesn't give or care as much for me." "I live with my mother and she is always telling me what to do with my baby" (see Table 1).

The majority of the respondents indicated their problems were better since the initial impact of becoming a mother. This could be attributed to support services they were receiving and/or the process of role adaptation. In other words, stress and anxiety, due to the major change in their lives, was reduced over time. Another plausible explanation of improvement of problems may be the result of support and encouragement from family members.

Table 1

Most Difficult Problems of Adolescent Mothers

Problems Rank Ordered	1st		2nd		3rd		Weighted Rank Ordered+
	N	%	N	%	N	%	
Change in priorities	4	20.0	3	15.0	1	5.0	19*
Increased responsibilities	4	20.0	3	15.0			18**
Independence vs. dependence	4	20.0	1	5.0			14***
Lack of family support	2	10.0	2	10.0	1	5.0	11
Decreased self-attention	2	10.0	1	5.0	1	5.0	9
Decreased concentration	1	5.0	1	5.0			5
Finding a house/apartment	1	5.0					3
Self-satisfaction			1	5.0			2
None	2	10.0					
Other°			8	40.0	17	85.0	

N = 20

°Other indicates: does not apply/no response.

+In order to define more clearly the ranking and intensity of the problems, the following procedure was incorporated: the frequency of responses x the multiplier (constant).

Significantly, the problems most frequently cited by less than one-half of the respondents as not getting any better were: a change in priorities with less free time; increased responsibility; and decreased concentration, especially with school work. This finding suggests these consumers are maintaining their responsibilities of parenting and realizing that the care of an infant is not an easy task but a responsibility they must perform while adhering to their own personal, educational, and social needs. Also as the infant gets older and mobility increases, the demands on the mother's time tend to increase. Therefore, the finding seems to indicate that the respondents' perceptions of their situation is reality-based.

In addition to these responses, the adolescent mothers identified, in ranked order, the following persons as most helpful to them with their life events: self, the father of their child, and mother/grandmother. The emphasis on self suggests the importance of self-sufficiency and a move toward interdependence. It also suggests there is acceptance by the adolescent mother of the importance of carrying out the maternal and other related roles, especially if she perceives her role as key in resolving the identified problems. It is worth noting that the child care and parenting program, where the interviews took place, encouraged the participation of fathers; the staff was not oblivious to the father's role not to the importance of mother-daughter relationships.

Overall, these findings suggest that individual consumer respondents were developing a sense of self-identity and forming meaningful personal relationships outside of their immediate family. Yet these adolescents acknowledged the value of their mothers helping them to deal with this new role and the responsibilities inherent in being a mother. This is an important consideration for program planning and program content for agencies need to recognize the importance of family contact and involvement.

3. Perception of Needs

Each respondent was asked to identify the three most important services needed by adolescent mothers. They were then asked to rank them according to their preferences (see Table 2).

For a brief summary of the identified needs associated with services, a construction from the respondents' rank ordering as well as comments about the attributes of services proceed as follows: (1) There is a great need for sufficient funds to provide independent living for themselves and their babies, and to assist them in their ability to utilize services such as well-baby clinics, health care, and day care, to meet the underlying need for self-sufficiency and/or independence; (2) If the above circumstances are satisfied, a concentrated effort toward personal and interpersonal adjustment is possible with individual counseling. Counseling should be beneficial, not only to the adolescent mother but to her infant who depends on her strengths and well-being. (3) Feeling comfortable with herself and her infant's situation, the mothers's progress toward self-sufficiency must be continued and enhanced by continuing academic education. The extent to which the value of education is related to self-esteem and general peer competitiveness was not

Table 2

Services Most Needed by Adolescent Mothers

Type of Service Rank Ordered	1st		2nd		3rd		Weighted Rank Ordered+
	N	%	N	%	N	%	
Financial assistance	5	25.0	5	25.0	3	15.0	31*
Well-baby clinic	6	30.0	4	20.0	2	10.0	28**
Health care services	1	5.0	4	20.0	3	15.0	14***
Infant day care	3	15.0	1	5.0	2	10.0	13
Individual counseling	2	10.0	2	10.0	1	5.0	11
Academic education	2	10.0			4	20.0	10
Housing	1	5.0	1	5.0	2	10.0	7
Job placement			1	5.0	1	5.0	3
Recreation			1	5.0			2
Parenting education			1	5.0			2
Transportation					2	10.0	2

N = 20

+In order to define more clearly the ranking and intensity of the problems, the following procedure was incorporated: the frequency of response x the multiplier (constant).

probed. However, the developmental theory of the adolescent does suggest such a relationship exists. Housing, job placement, recreation, parenting education, and transportation also were identified needs.

A majority of these services have been utilized at some point by most of the adolescent mothers. The least frequently utilized was assistance with locating housing, since the majority (90 percent) live with their family of origin or relatives. This data suggests that health care is actually the most important service needed when special and general (primary) health care are combined. This finding reflects what adults tend to perceive as the most important needed service, and it is often a primary component of many comprehensive services programs.

Extent of Need Satisfaction

Following a ranking of the most important services needed, the adolescent mothers were asked whether the services met their needs and about their overall support systems. The majority (75 percent) of the adolescent mothers indicated the services they receive met their needs either often or somewhat.

The overall support system of the majority (60 percent) of adolescent mothers was describes as sufficient; 30 percent indicated it was somewhat sufficient. Prior to and after becoming a mother, 55 percent of the consumer respondents identified their mother as most supportive; 15 percent identified the father of their child as most supportive. The importance of both the adolescent's mother and father of her child is consistently indicated in this study, and deserves very careful attention from program developers. These significant others must be included in the provision of services, if the adolescent mother is to be understood, the satisfaction of her needs are to be maximized, and ultimately, effective services provided to her.

4. Perception of Services Utilized

This section focused on areas associated with enhancing motivation for agency or clinic visits and more importantly, return visits. The respondents were asked to identify and describe what they considered as the three most important aspects of a service.

Highlighted in this section is the rank ordering (see Table 3) of

Table 3

Most Valued Aspects of a Service

Valued Aspects Rank Ordered	1st		2nd		3rd		Weighted Rank Ordered+
	N	%	N	%	N	%	
Respect	8	40.0	1	5.0	4	20.0	30*
Accurate information	4	20.0	6	30.0			24**
Appropriate questions	2	10.0	2	10.0			10***
Adequate service	2	10.0	1	5.0			8
To be seen immediately			3	15.0			6
Communication	1	5.0	1	5.0	1	5.0	6
Clean surroundings	1	5.0			1	5.0	4
Client participation			1	5.0			2
No response	2	10.0	5	25.0	14	70.0	

N = 20

+In order to define more clearly the ranking and intensity of the problems, the following procedure was incorporated: the frequency of response x the multiplier (constant).

the three most important aspects of a service. These evaluative aspects are based on the experiences these adolescent mothers had with services they utilized and many of which they continue to utilize. Respect, accurate information, and appropriate questions ranked highest.

The following aspects of service with typical comments by these consumers are:

1. *Lack of Respect and Consideration:* "They (staff) should be polite and courteous. It is the way they talk to you." "Staff should not act like they are better than you. They should respect you as a human being and show consideration." "The attitudes should be pleasing . . . the staff should be pleasing."
2. *Lack of Accurate Information:* "They (staff) should let you know what the service is about. The should be up front about it." "The people working there should know what they are doing." "Staff should give clear and accurate explanations about what they are doing."
3. *Inappropriate Questions:* "They ask a lot of personal, seemingly unnecessary questions." "I don't like being asked questions, given advice, or suggestions that are not a part of their job."

Services Emphasized

The adolescent mothers were asked what services they most frequently used. The findings in Table 4 reflect the services which respondents identified as the most and least interesting services they received.

The largest number of respondents (30 percent) reported parenting education as the most interesting. Some typical comments are: "They are concerned about us and spend time with us." ". . . talking with peers about different experiences with their babies. . . ." "I am learning about caring for my baby." The next most interesting service, mentioned by 25 percent of the respondents, was infant day care. "I like the way they communicate with the babies. The baby is more responsive." "I like the atmosphere and the care given my baby."

An equal distribution (15 percent) of the respondents identified the well-baby clinic and child care services as most interesting. Academic education was slated by 10 percent of the respondents and financial assistance indicated by 5 percent as the most interesting service.

The most frequently mentioned service that was identified as least interesting by 30 percent of the respondents was public assistance. A typical comment by one respondent was: "It's confusing. They lose items, give inaccurate information and they are not very efficient." Fifteen percent of the respondents identified the well-baby clinic as least interesting, commenting, for example: ". . .

Table 4

Most and Least Interesting Services

Most Interesting Service Rank Ordered			Least Interesting Service Rank Ordered		
	N	%		N	%
Parenting education	6	30.0	Financial Assistance	6	30.0
Infant day care	5	25.0	Well baby clinic	3	15.0
Well baby clinic	3	15.0	Academic education	2	10.0
Child care services	3	15.0	Child care services	2	10.0
Academic education	2	10.0	Parenting education	2	10.0
Financial assistance	1	5.0	Public transportation	1	5.0
			Gynecological services	1	5.0
			Family planning	1	5.0
			No response	2	10.0

spend several hours just sitting." "There is too much time wasted just sitting in the waiting room."

Again an equal distribution (10 percent) of respondents identified the following services as least interesting: academic education, child care services, and parenting education. One respondent made the following comment about academic education: ". . . boring, not challenging, too easy. . . ." A very brief but blunt comment about child care services was, "rather boring." The following services were identified by one respondent (5 percent) each as least interesting: public transportation, gynecological services, and family planning.

In review of services emphasized, the most interesting services identified strongly suggest that the extent to which the consumer is involved in an agency depends on the attitudes an agency's personnel project and the quality of care given. This certainly includes the adolescent mothers' understanding of what is happening as they are processed through the agency.

On the other hand, the least interesting services identified by the respondents strongly reflects a lack of involvement due to negative attitudes, questionable quality of care, lack of understanding, and perceived lack of concern by agency personnel. For the respondents, the emphasis tended to be on adequate services and the overall quality of care within those services.

The majority (85 percent) of respondents said they intended to complete the service or program they identified as least interesting, while only one (5 percent) said she did not intend to finish the program. The percent did not identify any services as least interesting. A qualitative composite view of the most important findings in this study is presented in the summary of Consumer Responses in Table 5.

DISCUSSION AND IMPLICATIONS

This chapter reports the findings of a study descriptive and exploratory in scope. The perceptions of adolescent mothers' problems, their needs and the services they received were identified and described by the young women themselves and suggested the extent of utilization of these services by these teen mothers. A major limitation of the study was the use of a nonrandom convenience sample of Black adolescent mothers who were selected from one agency. The findings and analysis could not be generalized to the general population of Black adolescent mothers. However, many of the findings give added support to existing recommendations stated or inferred by related studies and statistical reports, and provide useful information for the further development of research questions and hypotheses about adolescent mothers.

The findings are an important contribution to understanding adolescent mothers as a heterogeneous population; their individual perceptions and motivations are based on unique experiences and transactions within service delivery systems. This suggests a need for further in-depth studies that focus on the perceptions of the adoles-

Table 5

Summary of Consumer Responses

Identified problems	Change in priorities Increased responsibilities Independence vs. dependence
Most helpful person	Self Father of the child Mother or grandmother
Identified needs	Financial assistance Well baby clinics Health care services
Needs met through service provision	Somewhat to often
Quality of primary support systems	Sufficient to somewhat sufficient
Most supportive person before and after becoming a mother	Mother Father of the child
Reason for referral	Special problems with child Need for speciality clinics Added support Child care
Negative aspects of services received	Respect and consideration Accurate information Appropriate questions
Most interesting service	Parenting education Infant day care
Least interesting service	Financial assistance Well baby clinics
Overall evaluation of services	Need to improve the provision of adequate services and quality of care

cent mother as an individual, a parent, and a consumer of related services.

In addition, the results of the study suggest the potential contributions adolescent mothers can make to program planning and development for services to them. In this way they can contribute to their own social development. For example, the area of cooperative decision-making may enhance other social skills and productive capacity. However, incorporating the input of these consumers must be done without minimizing the contributions and existing roles of the providers, and of scientific and other professionals who must continue to be diligent in their roles as experts, supporters and advocates of this younger segment of the population. There is mutual benefit for all in the long run, especially in the social development of our future adult generations. In other words, the transactional processes occurring during service delivery are just as important as program content, for they relate closely to how these adolescent mothers view services. Services utilization is also very much affected.

Of the many implications — service delivery, research, theory, and policy — associated with the findings of this study, the emphasis in this chapter is how to minimize the negative consequences that can but do not have to result from adolescent motherhood. The focus is to increase the potential of adolescent mothers for self-sufficiency. Furthermore, the findings emphasize the need for comprehensive services that embrace positive strategies for social development. Implications that have relevance to this study are detailed here in terms of needs revealed:

1. A need to determine the acceptability of services to the consumer, thereby including the adolescent mother in the planning and decision-making process. One of the most striking findings related to this need is reflected in the comments made about the most and least interesting services; for example, attitudes that service providers or agency personnel project, and the quality of care given may affect the length and quality of consumer participation. Positive responses from the consumer suggested that learning and increased participation are most reflective of positive interactions within specific service agencies. On the other hand, the identified least interesting services strongly suggest a lack of involvement possibly due to perceived negative attitudes, poor quality of care, and a lack of understanding by agency personnel.

2. A need for comprehensive agency orientation for all new staff so clear and accurate communication can be enhanced. This is especially needed regarding aspects of client contact.

3. A need to provide ongoing in-service training for personnel

working with adolescent mothers to increase sensitivity and awareness of consumer perceptions. This is suggested from the existing literature as well as from the comments made by respondents. Emphasis on training pertaining to personnel of day care centers, public assistance programs, and educational institutions is needed.

4. A need for ongoing case management to identify areas or progress and the extent of need for appropriate intervention. A prior step should by to solicit the adolescent mother's input.

5. A need for community-wide educational activities and involvement, including family involvement, for the findings in this study suggest that consumers depend on persons in their natural environments. In addition, comments made by respondents suggest that they react to attitudes projected by others. The extent to which they are able to become self-sufficient and manage their own responsibilities will depend on the sensitivity accorded them.

This is an especially important implication in light of findings which indicate that adolescent motherhood is not necessarily a cross-generational pattern; living situations are not necessarily unsatisfactory or nonsupportive; and primary support usually comes from the mother of the adolescent and the father of her child.

CONCLUSION

To improve the effectiveness of service delivery, thus increasing the likelihood of a higher level of consumer utilization mutual interaction is essential between consumers and service providers. The social reality of adolescent mothers is based on their unique experiences and perceptions and involves such critical issues as the awareness and acceptance of differing value systems and the extent of their sharing in the planning and decision-making processes. Thus adolescent mothers may receive opportunities to develop necessary social skills and to be recognized as important and productive contributors of society who possess a sense of well-being and accomplishment. In the words of Jones and Pandey (1981) from *Social Development*:

The ultimate purpose of development is to provide increased opportunities to all people for a better life. . . . The shift of emphasis to social development from exclusively economic development refers to the process of planned institutional change to bring about a better correspondence between human needs on the one hand and social policies and programs on the other.

In this study, many of the adolescent mothers were involved in programs and activities to improve their sense of well-being and to formulate realistic goals that would enable them to become productive members of society. The mothers of adolescent mothers and the fathers of their children have been recognized as essential supports. These supports aid adolescents who are struggling with interdependence issues and conflicts, as well as with skills testing to develop their differing roles of individual and mother, while attempting to meet their psychological and social needs.

These adolescents have added to these difficult tasks the further responsibility of caring, sharing, and meeting the needs of a child of their own. Yet many adolescent mothers have a sense of being able to accomplish these formidable tasks; they see themselves as capable, responsible individuals.

The fear that adolescent motherhood is becoming a difficult and often intractable, aggregate social problem may be minimized with appropriate comprehensive services. Adolescent mothers require different levels of support, based on their individual needs. Therefore, they need the opportunity, encouragement, and support to realize successful accomplishments and to enhance their productive capacity, self-sufficiency, and self-determination.

REFERENCES

Bayh, B. (1976). Statement of Hon. B. Bayh, a U.S. Senator from the State of Indiana. *Hearings on S. 2538, The School Age Mother and Child Act of 1975*. Washington, DC: U.S. Government Printing Office, 544.

Bice, T. & White, K. (1971, May-June). Cross-national comparative research on the utilization of medical services. *Medical Care, 9,* 253-271.

Bilsborrow, L. E. (1977). *The long term effects of adolescent pregnancy and childbearing on women.* Chapel Hill, NC: University of North Carolina.

Bogue, D. (Ed.) (1977). *Adolescent fertility.* Chicago: Community and Family Study Center, University of Chicago.

Bolton, F. G. (1980). *The pregnant adolescent.* California: Sage Publications.

Bruce, J. (1978, January). Adolescent parents: A special case of the unplanned family. *The Family Coordinator,* 75-78.

Bureau of Community Health Services (1978). *Improving family planning services for teenagers.* Maryland: Department of Health, Education, and Welfare.

Card, J. & Wise, L. (1978, July-August). Teenage mothers and teenage fathers: The impact of early childbearing on the parents' personal and professional lives. *Family Planning Perspective, 10*(4), 199-205.
Consumer Health Perspective (1980, March). End of the decade: A consumer view. New York: Consumer Commission on the Accreditation of Health Services, Inc., 3.
DeLissovoy, V. (1973, July-August). Child care by adolescent parents. *Children Today, 2*(4), 22-25.
Forbush, J. B. (1981). Adolescent parent programs and family involvements. In Theodore Ooms (Ed.), *Teenage pregnancy in a family context: Implications for policy*. Philadelphia: Temple University Press, 254-276.
Forbush, J. & Leigh, B. (1977, March). *National directory of services for school-age parents*. Washington, DC: National Alliance Concerned with School Age Parents.
Fox, K. (1974). *Social indicators and social theory*. New York: John Wiley & Sons.
Furstenberg, F. (1976). The social consequences of teenage parenthood. *Family Planning Perspective, 8*, 1976.
Garber, S. (Ed.) (1978). Adolescence for adults. *A report by Blue Cross*.
Garbarino, J. (1981). Knowledge in the services of children and youth. *Children and Youth Services Review, 3*(4), 269-275.
Guttmacher, A. (1981). *Teenage pregnancy, the problem hasn't gone away*. New York: Alan Guttmacher Institute.
Guttmacher Institute (1976). *11 million teenagers*. New York: Alan Guttmacher Institute.
Jones, T. & Pandey, R. (Eds.) (1981). *Social development*. New York: St. Martins Press.
Massey, C. (1980, December). Consumer-provider health care roles. *Maternal/Newborn Advocate, 7*(3), New York: March of Dimes Foundations.
National Association of Social Workers (1982, January). Editorial comment. *Social Work in Education, 4*(2), 4.
National Center for Health Statistics (1978). Monthly vital statistics: Report No. 10. Maryland: U.S. Health Services Natality Statistics.
Ogg, E. (1976). *Unmarried teenagers and their children*. Public Affairs Pamphlet, No. 537.
Paiva, J. F. X. (1981). Program planning. In T. Jones & R. Pandey (Eds.), *Social development*. New York: St. Martins Press.
Pandey, R. S. (1981). Strategies for social development. In T. Jones & R. Pandey (Eds.), *Social development*. New York: St. Martins Press, 39-41.
Reinhold, R. (1977, September 21). Birth rate among girls 15 to 17 rises in "puzzling" 10 year trend. *New York Times*.
Schwartz, B. A. (1981, February). Having a baby. *Journal of the Child Welfare League of America, Inc., VII*(2), 39.
Stouffer, S. (1962). *Social research to test ideas*. New York: The Free Press.
Trussell, J. (1976, July-August). Economic consequences of teenage childbearing. *Family Planning Perspectives, 8*(4), 184-190.

Adolescent Sexual Activity, Pregnancy, and Childrearing: Attitudes of Significant Others as Risk Factors

Robert C. Evans

ABSTRACT. Adolescent pregnancy has increased significantly within the last five years among Black adolescent females. Black adolescent mothers account for more than half of all births among Black women. The problems associated with adolescent pregnancy and childrearing are numerous, and it seems very worthwhile to assess how adolescent females are impacted by those people close to them, regarding sexual activity and having children. Hence, the present research focused on discerning the attitudes of significant others as targets (i.e., mother, father, male friends, female friends and teachers) and assessing those attitudes as risk factors associated with adolescent pregnancy and childrearing utilizing an exploratory, descriptive research design. Attitudinal factors were measured by a sexual permissiveness and pregnancy childrearing scale. The sample included 45 adolescent females between 16-17 years of age. Fifteen respondents who were sexually active but did not have a child, 15 were never sexually active, and 15 were rearing one child under two years of age. All the participants lived at home with their parent(s) and were currently enrolled in high school. Pencil and paper measures were used to collect the data in community-based health centers in Pittsburgh, Pennsylvania. The data revealed significant difference on each of the attitudinal factors among the three groups of targets, except that of male adolescent friends. These significant findings from such a small sample suggest that attitudinal risk factors are important in understanding causality and in implementing prevention

Robert C. Evans, CSW, ACSW, PhD, is Visiting Assistant Professor in the Loyola University of Chicago School of Social Work. He is currently engaged in a funded longitudinal study of family relationships and child behavior traits within families with a sickle cell child. The study described in this chapter was conducted as part of Dr. Evans' doctoral dissertation, School of Social Work, University of Pittsburgh, Pittsburgh, PA. Dr. Evans thanks Dr. Charlotte J. Dunmore, Chairperson, Dr. Jerome Taylor, Dr. Martha Baum, Dr. Jake Milliones, and Dr. Mary Page. Also special thanks to Dr. Helen L. Evans for editing assistance.

75

of adolescent pregnancy. The influence of female friends, mothers, and fathers is discussed as a critical component to any intervention strategies aimed at prevention.

Thirty million adolescents are estimated to be living in the United States, and about one out of every two aged 15-19 years is sexually active. One out of ten adolescents is likely to become pregnant, for single adolescent females between 15 and 19 years of age have accounted for about half of out-of-wedlock births (Guttmacher Institute, 1981). Further, the Guttmacher Institute (1981) reported that 96 percent of unmarried adolescent mothers keep their babies, and Blacks are more likely than Whites to keep their babies. Other authors in this text have commented on these facts. The professional literature has also proliferated: Furstenberg (1976), Juhasz (1974), and Klerman and Jekel (1973) have raised concerns about the negative social, psychological, and economic consequences of adolescents having and raising their own babies. These significant issues must be addressed through research *and* appropriate interventions.

Many studies (Freeman & Rickles, 1979; Fischman, 1977; Gottschalk, 1964; Gispert & Falk, 1976; and Clapp & Raab, 1978) have concluded that the adolescent who decides to keep her baby is distinctively different from other adolescent females. Clapp and Raab (1978) suggest that the expressed desire of adolescent females to rear their own children may be attributed to the impact of the "human rights movements, and increased openness on the part of the media in presenting sexual material and the diminished status of the traditional marriage" (p. 149).

It is apparent that adolescent females who keep their children are supported in this decision by their parents or by the baby's father (Fischman, 1977; Gispert & Falk, 1976; Clapp & Raab, 1978). Also adolescent females who keep their babies more frequently report that they desired to have a child as noted by Fischman (1977), Clapp and Raab (1978) and Zelnik and Kantner (1974). The latter observation is a shift from earlier findings which suggested that pregnancies were "unintended" and "unplanned" (Furstenberg, 1976; Zelnik & Kantner, 1972).

In the present study it was assumed the likelihood of an adolescent female's becoming sexually active, or having and keeping her baby might be influenced by her mother, father, male friends, female friends, and/or teachers. Within the context of this study, these persons are referred to as significant targets, for they have been found to be important in adolescent development (Baumrind, 1975; Blos, 1979 and 1962).

In looking at an adolescent female's chances of becoming sexually active, Sexton (1983) discovered that the sexual attitudes expressed by parents were more likely to influence the adolescent's becoming sexually active than the popular media. In a study of low-income Black girls, Ladner (1971) reported that premarital sex was not regarded as an immoral act by the majority of the families in her study. Rather it was viewed as a "human function" believed to be a natural process. Bell (1966) studied how sexual values are transmitted, finding that if a strong emotional involvement prevailed between parents and their adolescent child, it would likely influence the teen's premarital sexual behavior. Adolescents may be more inclined to engage in sex, which is highly attractive to them, if parental messages are not clear (Bell, 1966).

When comparing the attitudes of White middle-income mothers and their daughters on sexual behavior, LoPiccolo (1973) revealed that mother and daughter did not differ regarding premarital kissing and petting, but did disagree concerning full sexual intercourse (daughter accepting, mother not accepting). Spanier (1977) utilized a sexually mixed White middle-class college sample to investigate sexual behavior as a function of the source of sexual information, finding that sexual behavior of college females was influenced toward noninvolvement by their mothers and toward becoming sexually involved by male friends, and by reading about sex. This study supports the salience of mothers and male friends as definite influences on the sexual behavior of young females.

Spanier also reported that teachers contributed very little sexual information and had little impact on the sexual behavior of female college students. Fathers had even less influence than teachers and provided them with little sexual information. Spanier's findings regarding teachers and fathers are contrary to Ladner's (1971) observations which found the influence of both teachers and fathers as important regarding the girls' chances of becoming sexually active.

Ladner (1971) observed that adolescent females who engaged in premarital sex did so often as a result of discussions with their female peers and boyfriends. Ladner found as did Spanier (1977) that boyfriends usually pushed for sexual intercourse on several occasions before the adolescent female would consent. Many girls felt they could not stall or put their boyfriends off very long. Ladner

(1971) described this as a sense of powerlessness on the part of the young female, and this perception is supported by Furstenberg (1976) and Zelnik and Kantner (1972 and 1977).

The research noted suggests then that young females' sexual behaviors may be most influenced by their mothers, fathers, female friends, male friends and teachers. Little information was actually revealed regarding the influence of teachers but this author suspects teachers could have critical impact on the lives of low-income adolescent females.

A similar set of significant targets (mother, father, male friends, female friends, and teachers) is likely to influence the possibility of an adolescent female's becoming pregnant and keeping her baby. Is there a strong association between the values one places on childbirth and one's likelihood of getting pregnant (Ladner, 1971)? Townes et al. (1979) evaluated the extent to which a desire to have a family influenced a teenager's choice to have a child, or keep her child if she becomes pregnant. Townes and her associates also observed three major variables that impact on the risk of pregnancy: "liking kids, the influence of having a child on educational attainment and wanting to be a mother or father" (p. 23). Considering enjoying children as a risk factor parallels what Ladner (1971) and Stack (1974) found in their studies of two separate Black communities. This factor likely increases the chances that Black adolescent females will keep their babies.

Further, Ladner (1971) found that children born to single adolescent mothers were neither stigmatized nor viewed as mistakes. The community's accepting attitude helped the young adolescent mother to deal with her possible guilt about early childbirth. Grandparents usually reacted negatively when first hearing of a granddaughter's pregnancy but quickly learned to accept it (Ladner, 1971; Furstenberg, 1976). In a study of 62 Black pregnant adolescents, Held (1981) noted that adolescents rated their mothers as most disapproving and the fathers-to-be as most approving of their pregnancy. The adolescents also rank ordered respectively their mothers, fathers, themselves, and their baby's fathers as most important to them. Held additionally reported that teachers and other professionals were not ranked as important to the adolescents.

In an anthropological study, it was revealed that the Black families studied seemed to value childbirth and motherhood (Gabriel, 1983). This important message is communicated to adolescent females who verbalized that motherhood was a sign of adulthood and maturity. In another survey of 498 mid-Western shopping center patrons, Rinck et al. (1983) observed that 70 percent of the Black respondents favored an adolescent female's keeping her child if she became pregnant; only 5 percent mentioned abortion as a way to manage teenage pregnancy. In this same survey, single and separated respondents also felt a pregnant adolescent should keep her baby, as did a large percentage of high school respondents.

These findings indicate the value significant target figures may hold, for the targets' attitudes likely influence the decision an adolescent mother may make regarding whether to have and raise her baby. Significant interpersonal relationships of adolescent females then influence whether they become sexually active or have and keep their own babies. The current study was intended to provide further information delineating the impact mothers, fathers, male friends, female friends, and teachers have on the likelihood that an adolescent female will become sexually active, or have and keep her child. The approach rested upon evaluating the attitudes of significant targets.

METHODOLOGY

An exploratory design to produce quantitative descriptive data was formulated. Adolescent females voluntarily and anonymously completed questionnaires. Data were collected between November, 1979 and February, 1980.

Forty-five Black adolescent females participated in the study and were drawn respectively from a health maintenance organization (n = 16), a neighborhood family health center (n = 15), a social service agency for young women (n = 12), and a nontraditional health service clinic (n = 2). Participants were 16 and 17 years old, were attending high school, were residents of Pittsburgh, and lived at home with their parent(s) and had low incomes. The referring agencies verified that participants' family incomes were below or at the poverty level, that is, $8,000 to $9,000 for a family of four. Participants were stratified nonrandomly on childrearing status and sexual experience. Three groups of adolescents were defined: those having and rearing a child, those sexually active and never pregnant, and those never sexually active.

Potential subjects were asked by staff persons in the various agencies to engage in the study. When meeting the participants, the

researcher reiterated the nature of the study and mentioned that
results would be made available to them at a later date. Participants
were also asked to sign a consent form which indicated their volun-
tary participation and understanding of the purpose of the study. The
researcher remained with the participant(s) throughout the testing to
answer any questions or clarify aspects of the questionnaire, hoping
to ensure a high degree of test reliability.

Perceived attitudes toward adolescent sexual permissiveness, and
pregnancy and childrearing was measured by a ten-item scale (see
Table 1). The first five items examined adolescent sexual permissiveness and the second five adolescent pregnancy and childrearing.

Items measuring attitudes toward sexual permissiveness were
based on a revised Reiss Scale of Sexual Permissiveness by LoPiccolo (1973) and by Wagner et al. (1973), depicting six levels of
adolescent sexual activity. Each level of Wagner's scale was used
except the "no activity level." Items on adolescent pregnancy were
based on the work of Townes et al. (1979). She and her associates
found five of their twelve items significantly different in terms of
age and sex. Thus these items were used to construct the pregnancy
and childrearing index.

Participants rated attitudes of their mothers, fathers, male
friends, female friends, and teachers on individual pages in order to
reduce response biases.

RESULTS

The three research groups—childrearers, sexually active/never
pregnant, and never sexually active adolescent females—
significantly differed in their estimation of the attitudes of their significant targets (mother, father, female friends and teachers) toward
sexual activity, and pregnancy and childrearing. The one exception
was the male friend (see Table 2, Means of Perceived Sexual Permissiveness Attitudes). Table 3 reveals the one-way ANOVA statistics on the targets' sexual permissiveness mean scores across the
groups. Male friends achieved an F value of 1.23, p = .3022. Each
of the other targets achieved significant main effects for sexual permissiveness. Figure 1 graphically shows that the sexual permissiveness mean scores of mothers, teachers and fathers increased with the
sexual and childbearing experiences of the adolescent females. Figure 1 also reveals that each of the adult targets across the groups

Table 1

Attitude Toward Adolescent Sexual Permissiveness, Pregnancy, and Childbearing.

0	1	2	3	4	5	6	7	8
Never		Rarely		Sometimes		Often		Always
should		should		should		should		should

My _____ would say that:

_____ 1. Girls let boys they like touch their bodies.*

_____ 2. High school girls kiss guys they are dating.

_____ 3. A girl lets her boyfriend sexually arouse her with his hands.

_____ 4. When a girl is dating a boy she really likes, she lets him go all the way with her.

_____ 5. A girl has sex with more than one guy.

_____ 6. Unmarried teenage girls think about having children of their own.

_____ 7. Girls in love may become pregnant before they are 18 years old.

_____ 8. Girls may have a child as a teenager if they want to.

_____ 9. Girls under 18 who get pregnant have their babies.

_____ 10. Teenage girls who are mothers raise their own babies.

*This is the actual scale administered to the interviewees.

achieved lower mean scores than the peer targets. However, male friends achieved the highest mean scores.

Table 2 and Figure 1 also exhibit that those never sexually active respondents' mean estimates of their parents' attitudes toward adolescent sexual involvement were lower than the other two groups. Mean estimates of their parents' attitudes by the childbearers were the highest among the groups. The sexually active/never pregnant

Table 2

Means of Perceived Sexual Permissiveness Attitudes of Targets by Groups

	Groups		
Targets	Childrearers (n=15)	Sexually Active/ Never Pregnant (n=15)	Never Sexually Active (n=15)
Mother	17.06	10.80	6.00
Female Friends	21.93	21.46	13.33
Male Friends	24.86	29.40	29.53
Father	11.06	8.20	2.90
Teacher	15.26	10.60	6.20

Table 3

One-Way ANOVA: Perceived Sexual Permissiveness Attitudes of Targets Across Groups

Targets	F-value	P-value
Mother	9.12	.0005
Female Friends	5.68	.0066
Male Friends	1.23	.3022
Father	4.10	.0236
Teachers	5.40	.0082

Figure 1

Distribution of Means: Sexual Permissiveness Attitudes by Groups and Targets

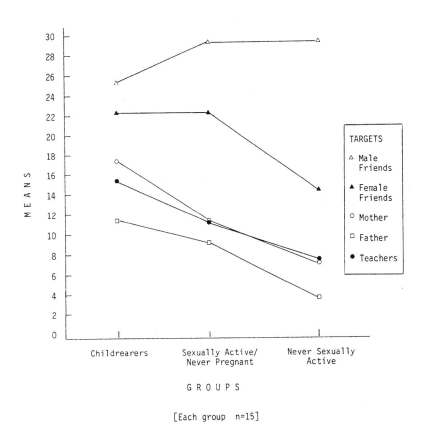

GROUPS

[Each group n=15]

respondents' mean estimates were in the middle. Moreover, the childrearers and sexually active/never pregnant subjects estimated their fathers' attitudes very similarly. The never sexually active group achieved the lowest mean scores across the groups regarding their fathers' and female friends' sexual permissiveness attitudes.

Table 4 reveals the groups' mean scores on pregnancy and child-birth attitudes. The means across the groups are lowest for fathers and highest for male friends, while Table 5 shows the one-way ANOVA statistics of the groups by targets on pregnancy/

Table 4

Means of Perceived Childrearing Attitudes of Targets by Groups

	Groups		
Targets	Childrearers (n=15)	Sexually Active/ Never Pregnant (n=15)	Never Sexually Active (n=15)
Mother	24.66	13.40	15.00
Female Friends	15.93	18.46	22.00
Male Friends	25.00	19.06	25.13
Father	21.06	8.53	11.06
Teachers	24.40	12.20	14.66

Table 5

One-Way ANOVA(s): Perceived Childrearing Attitudes of Targets Across Groups

Targets	F-value	P-value
Mother	15.27	.0000
Female Friends	5.99	.0051
Male Friends	3.10	.0552
Father	9.71	.0003
Teachers	10.98	.0001

childrearing attitudes. In Table 5, the groups' mean estimation of their male friends' attitudes toward adolescent females having a keeping their babies did not achieve statistical significant difference

(F = 3.10, p = .0552). Fathers of the adolescent females did achieve significant difference (F = 9.71, p = .0003). The location of the differences across the groups for fathers is revealed in Table 4; fathers' mean pregnancy/childrearing scores were highest for the childrearers and lowest for the sexually active/never pregnant respondents. The never sexually active group mean estimate of their fathers' attitudes was in the middle of the other two groups. Overall, the groups' mean childbearing attitude estimates, as exhibited in Table 4, were lowest for adults and highest for peers.

Given that Table 5 shows that each one-way ANOVA was significant — except for male friends — a look at Table 4 and Figure 2

Figure 2

Distribution of Means: Adolescent Sexuality and Childrearing Attitudes by Groups and Targets

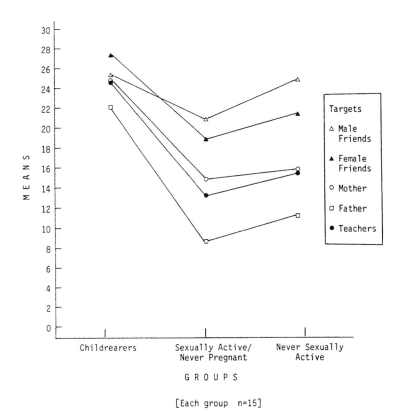

GROUPS

[Each group n=15]

reveals that childrearers, as opposed to the other two groups, accounted for the difference. The childrearers gave the highest mean estimates to each target except that of male friend. The other two groups produced similar estimates of their targets' attitudes, giving low estimates of their adult targets and somewhat higher estimates of their peer targets.

DISCUSSION

Important questions were raised as a result of the findings.

Sexual Permissiveness Attitudes

1. What does it mean to find a parallel relationship between the sexual activity of adolescent females and their estimates of the sexual permissiveness attitudes of their mothers and teachers?

This finding may very well reflect adolescent females' need to perceive their significant adult targets as supportive of their behavior. Given the design of the study which allows for the comparison of two sexually active groups to a nonactive group, this interpretation is likely to be valid. Sexton (1983) observed similarly that parental acceptance of adolescent sexual activity influenced the likelihood of a girl's becoming sexually active. Bell (1966) also supports the conclusion that parents influence the premarital sexual behavior of their children. However, respondents in the current study who reported not ever having sexual involvement estimated their mothers as most nonaccepting, while those respondents who reported being sexually active viewed their mothers as more accepting. It is possible that adolescent females who perceive their mothers as somewhat approving of sexual activity are more likely to try sexual intercourse.

Even though Spanier (1977) and Held (1981) both argue that teachers do not make a significant impact on the sexual behavior of adolescent females, the current study found that this might not be the case. The extent of an adolescent's sexual involvement paralleled her estimates of her teachers' acceptance of adolescent sexual permissiveness. As Ladner (1971) reported, some low-income Black adolescent females may use their female teachers as role models, in addition to their female relatives.

Hence the sexual attitudes of mothers and teachers both were important to the sexual activity of the present sample of low-income Black adolescents. These teenagers might be at risk for sexual involvement when they perceive their mothers or teachers as somewhat accepting of adolescent sexual involvement.

2. Why would the never sexually active respondents achieve a significantly lower mean score on fathers' attitudes toward sexual permissiveness than the other two groups?

Generally, having a perception of one's father's views on sexual involvement seemed important as to whether the adolescent female was sexually active or not. Those females who were not sexually active almost unanimously estimated their fathers as totally against adolescent sexual permissiveness. The perceived strongly negative attitude of their fathers may be a deterrent to sexual involvement for these girls, and may indicate the critical nature of the father's role in shaping the sexual behaviors of daughters. This realization can encourage the push for fathers to become more active in providing feedback and guidance to their adolescent daughters regarding sexual activity.

Finding fathers important in regard to their adolescent daughters' sexual activity is contrary to an earlier observation by Spanier (1977). Spanier's primary estimate of the father's influence was the amount of information regarding sex he gave his daughter. Moreover, it is likely that Spanier's observation affirms that there is a deficit in the communication of sexual information between fathers and their daughters. If fathers were to become more involved with their daughters' sex education, there might be a reduction in adolescent pregnancy.

3. What does it mean for the sexually active adolescent female to have female friends that they perceived to be accepting of sexual permissiveness?

This finding is important for both of the sexually active groups perceived their female friends as accepting of sexual involvement. Females seem more attracted to other females who share their own values. In either case, having a female friend who supports sexual involvement seems to be highly correlated with being sexually active. This supports Ladner's (1971) report that the sexual behavior of her low-income adolescent female subjects was strongly influenced by their female friends. Generally, peers have been found to be very influential in shaping the kinds of behaviors adolescents demonstrate. Interestingly, the never sexually active subjects perceived their female friends as not accepting of adolescent sexual involvement.

Pregnancy and Childbirth Attitudes

4. What might have caused the childrearers to estimate the pregnancy/childrearing attitudes of their mothers, fathers and teachers significantly higher than the other two groups?

Is this an acceptance of the fact that a child had been born? Maybe no one wished for the pregnancy but once the child was born, parents and teachers were perceived as accepting of both events. However, one may interpret the findings to mean that childrearers were at greatest risk for pregnancy and subsequent birth *because* their parents and teachers were perceived as supportive of those events. Given the current research design and levels of statistical significance between the groups on childbirth attitudes, the latter seems to be the most appropriate argument.

Pregnancy and childbirth may indeed occur as a result of adolescents perceiving their mothers and teachers as favoring these activities. This interpretation is consistent with Ladner's (1971) finding that having a child was valued by her low-income Black respondents, and also fits with the observations of Townes and her associates (1979), who found a positive relationship between wanting a child and subsequent pregnancy. As Gabriel (1983) found, Blacks value having children which makes the issue of adolescent pregnancy larger than that of adolescent females who become pregnant. Perhaps one way to counteract the possibly negative impact of valuing childbirth is to advocate that adolescents consider having children only when their life conditions are appropriate for the health and growth of a child. This is a major task in the Black community, when life conditions are relatively unstable or inadequate. Unemployment, poor education, poor housing and other problems affect Blacks of all ages and postponing childbirth is thus an issue for most Blacks.

5. What does it mean that the sexually active/never pregnant group estimated the attitudes of their female friends regarding pregnancy and childrearing significantly lower than the childrearers?

Adolescents who were sexually active but never pregnant may have been at less risk of becoming pregnant than the childrearers. It seems that the sexually active/never pregnant group was supported in their sexual behavior by their female friends. These friends (same sex peers) may be the most consistent source of social and emotional support for adolescent females (Ladner, 1971), and are likely to be a very significant influence in the development of young females. Interestingly, female friends were estimated by childrearers to be supportive of having children. If these positive attitudes of females are indeed a critical risk to becoming pregnant, then interventions should be focused in this direction, that is, adolescent females should be helped to support each other in not becoming pregnant.

Across Measures Comparisons

6. When comparing the sexual permissiveness and pregnancy/ childrearing mean scores of the childrearers, parents and teachers can be seen as accepting of sexual permissiveness. What does this mean?

There appears to be an inconsistency in the attitudes of the adult targets. Adolescent childrearers may be influenced by their parents and teachers who support giving birth while opposing sexual involvement. To value one and not the other communicates a mixed message to teenage girls. As Bell (1966) found, these ambivalent messages may place the adolescent at risk for pregnancy. Ladner (1971) and Furstenberg (1976) also observed that Black mothers of pregnant adolescents usually disapproved of sexual intercourse but approved having and keeping one's own child. Perhaps the Black community will continually deal more systemically and effectively with inconsistent values about sexuality and having children values that young people receive from their parents. The means to accomplish this needs the collective thinking of Black leaders and institutions.

7. The sexually active/never pregnant adolescents gave similar atttitudinal estimates on both the sexuality and childrearing measures for their significant adult targets. Why?

Does this indicate that sexually active/never pregnant respondents received consistent messages about childbirth and sexual permissiveness? It does seem they chose to become sexually active. This finding does not confirm Bell's (1960) notion that inconsistent parental messages about sex may cause an adolescent to become sexually active. There must be some other explanation for why adolescents become sexually active. Female friends, as stated above, are more salient to the adolescent's decision to engage in sex. The sexually active/never pregnant group may have been the least at risk for adolescent childbirth because their parents and teachers were perceived to hold consistent views on sexual involvement and pregnancy. Moreover, their female friends were not accepting of adolescents having children which also reduced their chances of becoming adolescent mothers.

8. The never sexually active respondents—though their mean score estimates were low on both measures—perceived their targets as more accepting of pregnancy and childrearing than of sexual permissiveness. What does this mean?

Adolescents who never had sexual intercourse could be at risk of becoming pregnant because of the perceived inconsistent messages given to them by their significant adult and peer targets. Unless there are other factors such as positive self-esteem to reduce the risk of pregnancy, this group may be in need of critical intervention to prevent pregnancy. Perhaps participation in female discussion groups that focused on sexual concerns would be beneficial.

9. What does it mean to have each of the adolescent female groups to estimate their male friends as accepting of adolescent sexual permissiveness and pregnancy?

Females in all the groups viewed their adolescent male friends very similarly. Adolescent males have been reported as the participant in adolescent heterosexual relationships who pushes for sexual intercourse (Ladner, 1971; Spanier, 1977). They also have been found to be very approving of pregnancy and childbirth (Held, 1981). As the groups' perceptions of males do not vary, the possible impact of males on the females is about the same. Thus the male adolescent target may not be as much of a risk factor in adolescent pregnancy or female sexual involvement as popular notions would have it. The perceived role of the male, even though stereotypical, seems to be very well identified by most of the respondents.

CONCLUSION

Helping to address and prevent adolescent pregnancy is a real challenge to human service professionals. The incidence of teen pregnancy is not lessening and there is need for sexual and pregnancy prevention work with adolescents and their significant targets. Three major conclusions have been drawn from the current study. First, the present research found that perceived attitudes of the adolescent female's mother, father, female friends, and teachers played a significant role in distinguishing those females who were childrearers, sexually active/never pregnant and never sexually active. Statistically, the chosen targets had varying degrees of importance in differentiating the adolescents.

However, the perceived attitudes of male friends did not achieve statistical significance. Male friends were perceived by each group of adolescent females as accepting of sexual involvement and childbirth. It seems that this level of similarity across the groups would indicate that male friends may not have differential influence on adolescent females. Thus even though males are necessary actors in causing adolescent pregnancy, they seem to be less important in influencing whether a female is sexually involved or an adolescent mother. Moreover, the perceived attitudes of female friends and significant adults achieved levels of statistical differences between the groups that would suggest they are influential actors in whether a female becomes sexually active or has and keeps her child.

The theoretical significance of female friends as an influence on the female adolescent's sexual involvement seems evident. The sexually active/never pregnant adolescents gauged their female friends as not accepting of adolescent pregnancy. The never sexually active adolescents saw their female friends as not accepting of sexual permissiveness, while the childrearers perceived their female friends as accepting of both sexual permissiveness and having children. In each instance, female friends were identified as holding an attitude consistent with the adolescent female's sexual and/or childbirth status. This suggests that adolescent females are influenced by the beliefs of their girlfriends. The critical importance of peer groups in shaping the values and behaviors of individual group members has been documented. Female peer group influence points to the essential need for intervention at this level to help groups of girls support themselves in refusing to become sexually active or pregnant.

The second major finding of the present study flows from the perceptions respondents had of their fathers. Fathers were seen, across the groups, as not approving of adolescent childbirth and sexual permissiveness. Significantly, the one group of adolescents that reported never having had sexual intercourse estimated their fathers as most nonaccepting of sexual involvement. It would seem that fathers did influence the sexual behavior of their daughters.

There has not been much attention given to how fathers influence the sexual behaviors of their adolescent daughters.

It is likely that a father's clear, firm and discouraging message — coming from this important male — regarding sexual involvement may reduce the likelihood of an adolescent's becoming sexually active. This doesn't mean that mothers and teachers are not significant in the resolution of early adolescent sexual involvement; the intent here is to highlight the importance of the father's role in shaping the sexual values and behaviors of his daughter. Human service providers need to highlight this role when counseling teenagers and/or their parents. Additionally, the electronic and print media need to become sensitive to and dramatize the role of fathers in adolescent female sexual development.

A final observation can be drawn from the current study relating to the kind of attitudinal messages adolescent females receive regarding pregnancy, childbirth, and sexual involvement. Child-rearers received the most inconsistent messages about these essential aspects of life. They perceived their mothers and teachers as accepting of childbirth but not of sexual involvement. This message may cause a double bind for some adolescents. Adolescents may not know what is appropriate and may not make the best decision when confronted with sexual intimacy. The inconsistency that mothers and teachers present may relate to their own female status or the larger community's inconsistent values. The Black community needs to evaluate its values regarding sexual expression and childbirth as well as the consequences of changes in these values. Adolescent pregnancy is a very important topic for Black researchers to investigate, for it is not only a social issue but a political and a moral concern as well.

REFERENCES

Baumrind, D. (1975). The contributions of the family to the development of competence in children. *Schizophrenia Bulletin, 14,* 12-37.
Bell, R. K. (1966). Parent-child conflict in sexual values. *Journal of Social Issues, 22,*(2), 34-44.
Blos, P. (1962). *On adolescence.* New York: The Free Press of Glencoe, Inc.
Blos, P. (1974). *The adolescent passage.* New York: International Universities Press, Inc.
Clapp, D. & Raab, R. (1978). Follow-up of unmarried adolescent mothers. *Social Work, 23*(2), 149-153.
Fischman, S. (1977). Delivery or abortion in inner city adolescents. *American Journal of Orthopsychiatry, 47*(1), 127-133.

Freeman, E. & Rickles, K. (1979). Adolescent contraceptive use: Current status of practice and research. *American Journal of Obstetrics and Gynecology, 53*(3), 388-394.

Furstenberg, F. (1976). *Unplanned parenthood – social consequences of teenage childbearing.* New York: The Free Press.

Gabriel, A. & McAnarney, E. (1983). Parenthood in two subcultures: White middle-class couples and Black low-income adolescents in Rochester, New York. *Adolescence, 18*(71), 595-608.

Gispert, M. & Falk, F. (1976). Sexual experimentation and pregnancy in young Black adolescents. *American Journal of Obstetrics and Gynecology, 126,* 459-466.

Gottschalk, L., Titchener, J. & Piker, H. et al. (1964). Psychosocial factors associated with pregnancy in adolescent girls. *Journal of Nervous and Mental Disease, 138,* 524-534.

Guttmacher Institute. (1981). *Teenage pregnancy: The problem that has not gone away.* New York: Planned Parenthood Federation of America, Inc.

Held, L. (1981). Self-esteem and social network of young pregnant teenagers. *Adolescence, 16*(64), 905-912.

Juhasz, A. M. (1974). The unmarried adolescent parent. *Adolescence, 9,* 263-272.

Klerman, L. & Jekel, J. (1973). *School age mothers.* Hamden, Connecticut: Linnet Books.

Ladner, J. A. (1971). *Tomorrow's tomorrow: The Black woman.* New York: Doubleday and Company, Inc.

LoPiccolo, J. (1973). Mothers and daughters: Perceived and real differences in sexual values. *The Journal of Sex Research, 9*(2), 171-177.

Rinck, C., Rudolph, J. A. & Simkins, L. (1983). A survey of attitudes concerning contraception and the resolution of teenage pregnancy. *Adolescence, 18*(72), 923-929.

Spanier, G. B. (1977). Sources of sex information and premarital sexual behavior. *The Journal of Sex Research, 13*(2), 73-88.

Sexton, D. L. F. (1984). Television sexuality, parental involvement and adolescents' sexual attitudes and behavior: A preliminary investigation. *Dissertation Abstracts International, 44*(7B), 2127B.

Stack, C. B. (1974). *All our kin.* New York: Harper & Row.

Townes, B. D., Wood, R. J., Beach, L. R. & Campbell, F. L. (1979). Adolescent values for childbearing. *The Journal of Sex Research, 15*(1), 21-26.

Wagner, N., Fujita, B. N. & Ronald, P. (1973). Sexual behavior in high school: Data on a small sample. *The Journal of Sex Research, 9*(2), 150)155.

Zelnik, M. & Kantner, J. (1977). Sexual and contraceptive experiences of young unmarried women in the U.S., 1966-1971. *Family Planning Perspectives, 9*(2), 55-73.

Zelnik, M. & Kantner, J. (1972). Sexual experiences of young unmarried women in the U.S. *Family Planning Perspectives, 4*(4), 9-18.

Black Adolescent Mothers and Their Families: Extending Services

Patricia J. Dunston
Gladys Walton Hall
Claudia Thorne-Henderson

ABSTRACT. This chapter addresses the impact the Black adolescent mother and her child have on their family, and reviews the literature on programs that serve adolescent mothers. The review indicates that the adolescent is usually viewed as the primary client; few efforts have been made to focus on the family in rendering services. A pilot program including the families of Black adolescent mothers is discussed here to highlight strategies for providing services within a family context. Barriers to providing services to families are also explored. Finally, a continuum indicating the range of services that can be provided to adolescent mothers and their families is proposed.

In the past, births by Black adolescents largely contributed to the rise of births to teenagers under 18 years old. Now this rise is more realistically viewed as a function on increased birth rates across all races. Yet while birth rates for Black teenagers have noticeably de-

Patricia Dunston, PhD, is Assistant Professor, School of Social Work, Howard University. Her private practice emphasizes family therapy with minority families, and her research has been in mental health and social issues as they relate to Black women. She serves on the Board of Examiners for Psychologists in Washington, DC, and is past president of the DC chapter of Black psychologists. Her publications include (co-editor) *Mental Health and People of Color.* Gladys Walton Hall, MSW, PhD, is Assistant Professor, School of Social Work, Howard University, teaching in the direct services sequence. She has chaired this sequence and been Assistant Dean. Dr. Hall has been a consultant with public and private agencies; she maintains a private practice. Her research focuses on childhood depression. Claudia Thorne-Henderson, BA, is Coordinator of the Child Health Improvement Project at Cities In Schools Adolescent Health Center, Washington, DC. She serves on a number of advisory boards and committees that address teenage pregnancy and is currently a masters degree candidate at Howard University School of Social Work. The authors gratefully acknowledge the professional assistance of Althea Truitt, Executive Director, Associated Catholic Charities, in the development of this chapter.

95

clined over the years, their rates still remain consistently higher than those for White adolescents. Statistics from 1979 and 1981 buttress this statement: In 1979, 92 percent of non-White births were Black (Baldwin, 1982), and 1981, 66.9 percent of Black births were to adolescents between the ages of 15-17 (National Center for Health Statistics [NCHS], 1983).

While there is public and professional acknowledgement that teenage childbearing is by no means solely a Black problem, the complexities of the problem for Black teenagers are great and clearly have been misunderstood. Black adolescents begin child-bearing at younger ages and experience more second and subsequent births than other races do. In 1981, Black adolescents, aged 15-17, had a higher percentage of second and subsequent births than any racial group (NCHS, 1983). These data suggest that Black adolescents are more likely to carry out parenting roles for two or more children while they are still adolescents.

The consequences of teenage childbearing have been fairly well documented, decreased educational and occupational attainment among them (Baldwin, 1982; Flaherty, Marecek, Olser & Wilcove, 1983). These consequences are compounded for Black adolescents. They generally do not have a spouse to contribute to their child's welfare. In 1981 only 33 percent of Black women, 15 years and older were married and living with spouses. Similarly, the educational level able to be attained by Black women as a group places them at the lower rungs of the ladder of success. Black women tend to be lowest in earning power compared to men and women both Black and White (Jones, 1983).

Adolescent mothers most often raise their children within the home of their family of origin. With the exception of a few studies (Furstenberg, 1976, 1981(a), 1981(b); Harper 1981), little is known about the sequence of events within the family from discovery of an adolescent's pregnancy to the positioning of the adolescent mother's child within the family of origin. Such insight is needed and becomes even more critical to the understanding of the plight of the Black adolescent's transition to motherhood.

Unfortunately, Black adolescent mothers will most likely be in a home where the economic situation is much worse than White adolescent mothers will experience. The 1980 median income of Black families was $12,674, compared to $21,904 for White families. Additionally, about 29 percent of Black families were below the poverty level, and 31 percent of those living in Black family households had incomes below the poverty level (Jones, 1983). Moreover, there is a greater probability Black families will have to face the responsibility for caring for an adolescent daughter and her child. When it comes to these families, few systematic, programmatic efforts have been mobilized to channel resources to the entire family. The adolescent mother is usually viewed as the client in need, when in reality the entire family may be a more appropriate focus for services.

For these reasons and others, that will be brought out, we have chosen to focus on the Black adolescent mother. Hence, this chapter addresses the Black adolescent mother's impact on her family, and raises concerns and strategies for adopting a family perspective in the delivery of services. The benefits of providing services from a family perspective will be assessed in light of one of the author's work with a pilot project that serviced Black adolescent mothers and their families. Discussion on services needs to include but not be limited to: (1) program limitations; (2) providers' perceived lack of motivation to work with Black families; and (3) the inclination of providers to focus on individuals rather than on families. Prior to our conclusions, we will incorporate a set of strategies for enhancing work with Black adolescent parents from a family perspective.

THE BLACK ADOLESCENT MOTHER'S IMPACT ON THE FAMILY

Teenage pregnancy is not exclusively a Black problem but as Butts (1981) has so eloquently stated, it has been the Black adolescent mother who "epitomizes the crux of the problem." The problem is her perceived dependency on welfare, and for Black women, the issue of dependency has been a dual societal dilemma. Dating back to the Moynihan Report (Moynihan, 1965), Black female-headed households have been singled out as perpetuators of problems within the Black community. Public attitudes as reflected in Placek and Hendershot's (1974) "brood sow" theory, characterize Black adolescent mothers as lower-class women who have children in order to qualify for welfare, and continue to have them in order to increase their welfare monies.

The more recent public focus on teenage pregnancy, and the consistently high rates of Black teenage births has heightened the concern that Black women are perpetuating a cycle of single-parent households. This misplaced concern ignores the fact that Black adolescent mothers comprise a small number of welfare recipients compared with the total welfare population (Bolton, 1980). Most importantly, such concern detracts from the strengths of these Black families and their ability to adapt to and accept various dependencies within the family. Focusing on the Black adolescent mother *and* her family has become even more critical (Chilman, 1984).

Extended caregiving among Blacks has been fairly well documented in the literature (Billingsly, 1968; Jeffers, 1967; Stack, 1974; McAdoo, 1978). Hill (1972) estimated that a large percentage of out-of-wedlock Black babies were absorbed within existing Black families instead of being given up for adoption. This incorporation of mother *and* child into her family of origin has its benefits and drawbacks. Reporting on a three-year follow-up sample of predominantly Black adolescent mothers, Presser (1980) found that 25 percent were living as single parents with their mothers. Mothers were giving their daughters child care, financial, and emotional support. Similarly, Miller (1983) found family members the predominant care providers to the adolescent mother's child. Colleta and Gregg (1979) also observed that Black adolescent mothers heavily depend on their own mothers for various resources.

Those adolescent mothers who felt supported by their families felt more positively toward their babies, were more highly motivated to complete their education, and felt better about themselves. Such support cushions the trauma associated with out-of-wedlock status. However, as noted by Presser (1980), the sharing of childrearing responsibilities among adolescent mothers, their mothers, and other relatives raises significant policy and research concerns. Little is known unfortunately about the psychological, economic, and social stresses brought on individual family members.

In Smith's (1975) study of Black grandmothers, it was acknowledged that the grandmothers were not eager to accept the role of childrearer for their daughter's child. These Black grandmothers were quite often young women themselves who foreseeably did not want the label "grandmother" at an early age. In addition, it is apparent their daughter's circumstances quite often recalled their own earlier experiences as adolescent mothers. Bolton (1980) also suggested that the woman placed in this situation will not embody the traditional grandmother role. He acknowledged possible interference to the adolescent mother's freedom to play the maternal role for her child due to her mother's presence.

Several other family dynamics can come into play (Furstenberg, 1976, 1980). The young Black mother often receives an elevated

position within the family: She is treated as an adult when she becomes a parent. Consequently, conflict may arise between the adolescent mother and her siblings who may become envious of this
treatment. Further, the grandmother's caregiving focus may be
drawn to sharing responsibilities with her daughter who is now a
mother; attention may be taken from the grandmother's other children. Also while the daughter may be elevated to the role of adult, is
she ready to assume this status?

The data from these other studies reveal that compared to their
nonpregnant peers, pregnant adolescents had lower self-esteem,
greater feelings of worthlessness, were more defensive, and experienced more conflict with their families. However, a major drawback
of this research rests in its inability to determine whether these characteristics were present before or as a consequence of the pregnancy.
As acknowledged by Bemis, Diers, and Sharpe (1976) normal concerns about defining one's identity can become extremely complicated by the time and energy consumed in fulfilling the responsibilities of early parenting. Inconsistent child care often results. This
situation inevitably impacts on the family.

Relationships among Black adolescent mothers and their families
then have been little written about or addressed in depth by service
providers. They provide no substantive indication of the psychological, social, and economic stresses of Black families. The literature
does, however, provide evidence for the increasingly important role
played by Black families in the childrearing of their adolescents'
children. Unfortunately, most studies use the teenager as the focus,
not the family constellation. The Black adolescent mother and child
are inseparable components of their family. The literature too
closely reflects the bias and limitations of services for adolescent
mothers, that is, dwelling on the adolescent — not her and her family. There is a need to know how Black families guide their own
development, stabilization, dissolution and incorporation of the new
child into the family constellation. This knowledge will help human
service professionals focus appropriate attention on the family in
rendering services.

SERVICE TO TEENAGE MOTHERS:
AN ASSESSMENT

Across the country, programs to serve adolescent mothers have
increased steadily from approximately 250 in 1970 to about 1,500 to
date. These agencies, located in urban and rural areas, serve girls of

different races and economic classes. In the large metropolitan areas, however, programs serve predominantly Black low-income adolescent mothers (Forbush & Maciocha, 1981). With the proliferation of programs, many vital services are now being provided to these youngsters. Yet it is not surprising that many improvements are needed within the service delivery system.

First, the services offered by most agencies tend to be narrow in focus, for example, providing only day care, medical care, or job training. However, the needs of adolescent mothers are multifaceted. Forbush and Maciocha (1981) provided a list of 42 services offered by agencies to illustrate the variety and extent of what adolescent mothers need. Miller (1983) reported that adolescent mothers use at least 15 services simultaneously. Hence the adolescent mother must be involved with several different agencies to have her needs met. Unfortunately, very few agencies offer a comprehensive approach to working with this population.

Another characteristic of programs serving adolescent mothers is that they generally utilize a crisis orientation model. Furstenberg (1976) concluded from his data on Black adolescent mothers that services offered to them produced short-term effects. The adolescent mothers were helped during pregnancy but abandoned when they became parents. Most programs regrettably and short-sightedly terminate services at a time when some of the gravest problems arise for adolescent mothers. Typically, many potential problems are ignored that may arise for the whole family when the adolescent mother and her child return to the family environment.

A third frustrating feature of existing programs is that funding is inadequate to reach a majority of the population in need (Moore, 1981). For example, it is estimated that sex education programs reach relatively few adolescents who are at serious risk for becoming pregnant (Sorenson, 1973; Zelnik & Kantner, 1980; Scales 1981). Similarly, educational programs for teenage mothers reach at most one-third of this population (Furstenberg, 1980). Funding is usually awarded for short periods of time, and the amounts awarded tend to vary a great deal from one year to the next (Forbush & Maciocha, 1981). Agencies are continually in the precarious situation of expending a tremendous amount of energy and time to fundraise. This time could go toward developing creative programs which could provide knowledge and services to all family members, not just the adolescent mother. The interrelatedness of these factors is quite obvious. Sufficient, consistent funding is a must if programs are to develop the comprehensive, long-term services needed for this multiproblem population and their families.

Quality of the programs serving adolescent mothers has been difficult to assess because few evaluation studies have been performed in this area (Forbush & Maciocha, 1981). Programs which have been assessed restricted outcome measures. Klerman's (1979) review of twenty-eight evaluation studies conducted since 1970 revealed that successful programs demonstrated only medical outcomes and educational achievements. Programs were not successful in reducing additional pregnancies; a very significant percentage of adolescents have another pregnancy within two years (Hertz, 1977; Biller, 1970; Bolton, 1980).

Forbush and Maciocha (1981) conducted one of the few surveys which explored the nature and extent of family involvement in service programs for teenage parents. Family involvement was defined as:

> . . . the extent to which program staff interview, consult with, and/or offer specific services to an adolescent girl's parents, sibling, or boyfriend and his family, and/or other family members. The contacts may be at the agency or in the homes of clients.

Very little has been done to incorporate a family perspective in service delivery. One of the authors here participated in the orchestration and implementation of a pilot program for adolescent teens *and* their families. Reviewing this program helps focus on the family perspective.

PARENT AIDE SUPPORT GROUP: A PILOT PROJECT

Discussion has focused on the lack of programmatic efforts to extend services to an adolescent mother's family. The pilot project presented in this section represents an exception to this rule. This experimental program, the Parent Aide Support Group, involved and rendered services to Black adolescent mothers *and* their families.[1] Developed by one of the authors of this chapter, it was a six-month project. Highlights of some of the unanticipated findings will be presented from this project that sought to:

1. Inform parents of the high-risk nature of teenage pregnancy, and sensitize parents to the emotional state of pregnant and parenting teens.
2. Alleviate the stress, guilt, and anger parents experience as a result of teenage pregnancy.
3. Strengthen the family structure; educate parents on the importance of being supportive so the family provides the pregnant or parenting teenager with the emotional support and resources necessary for her and her offspring to look forward to psychological, economic, and educational well-being.
4. Educate parents to be the primary sex educators of their children to prevent initial or subsequent pregnancies in adolescence.
5. Increase parental involvement in all phases of Cities In Schools[2] programming and service delivery.

The objectives were implemented by two parent support aides whose primary responsibilities were to provide services to parents and extended family members of adolescent mothers enrolled in the Washington, DC Cities In Schools program. The aides were recruited from the families of clients in the Cities In Schools program. They underwent 40 hours of classroom training for a two-month period to prepare for educating, providing information, and counseling Black adolescents' parents and extended family members.

Once the parent support aides completed the training program, and achieved competency in serving as resources to Black families, they began outreach to 50 family members in the Parent Aide Support Group. Outreach consisted of letter writing, phone calls and, most importantly, home visits. Initially, the aides implemented what was to be a series of ten guest-speaker forums on topics related to teenage pregnancy, including sex education, nutrition, prenatal care, and family and peer relationships.

However, the first forum drew low attendance with only three parents attending. These parents were spokespersons for the larger population of Black families. In reflecting on the low attendance, those parents that came surmised that Black parents' primary interests were to build marketable job skills and expand their own educational achievements. They expressed interest in adult education programs, receiving job referrals, and building career skills. They perceived that the problems of teenage pregnancy were secondary to their personal problems of unemployment, substandard housing, and desire for further education. The parents felt these areas should be addressed first, in addition to getting knowledge on teenage pregnancy and parenting.

These Black parents also explained that the low level of parental participation was not due to lack of concern for their daughters, nor did it reflect their own values regarding teenage parenting. It was due to feelings of inadequacy in a conference or learning situation, frustrations with lack of transportation and lack of appropriate clothing, uneasiness in group settings, and feelings of mistrust. They felt information shared in a group might be used against them while they were struggling to continue and/or secure social service assistance.

This invaluable input necessitated modifying the original program design. One-on-one family contact and group recreational activities proved less threatening to parents. Group social activities were implemented to address the parents' desire for continuing education and preparing for careers. These activities were coupled with family education topics such as adolescent development and sex education. Thirteen parents attended these activities and expressed interest in attending forums on a monthly basis. Several fathers requested that activities be planned when they were not obligated to work.

Through the one-on-one family contact, the parent support aides delivered a wide range of services to these families. One aide who regularly attended post-partum clinic with her own daughter functioned as a surrogate parent to clients who did not have strong or appropriate parent models at home. Through direct contact with families, the aides provided assistance to several families applying for services such as public assistance.

Further, the aides helped parents develop a support network to share transportation, babysitting and companionship to shut-ins and to those parents who needed more social outlets. Friendships evolved and emotional supports were established. Parents began to drop into the agency to get help from staff about other concerns and problems. The support aides conducted periodic orientations of the Cities In Schools Program, and two mothers began volunteering their time to the agency. As a result, the positive outcomes of the project did not only benefit the Black teenagers but had benefits for all family members.

Discussion of the Pilot Project

Several specific factors influenced increased participation in the program and should be highlighted, for they illustrate the strategies likely needed when services to adolescent mothers are broadened to include families. Before the project began, support aides were trained to develop skills needed to provide services from a family perspective. Thus changing the focus from the individual to the family will permit and encourage administrators of programs, it is hoped, to be aware of the skills of their workers, providing in-service training and ongoing consultation where needed.

Outreach to families was an essential feature of the pilot project. Home visits gave the support aides the opportunity to meet other family members; to explain personally the Parent Aide Support Group Project; and to help resolve problems which prevented parental attendance at forum meetings. Many of these problems were symptomatic of those faced in daily living, lack of transportation, babysitting, appropriate clothes, etc. The use of community residents to make home visits offers a viable strategy for providing vital outreach services.

Recognizing and responding to the need for program flexibility was another significant aspect of this project. When it was learned the original format was too structured and not meeting the needs of the parents, an informal and socially-oriented approach was adopted. This resulted in increased parental attendance and participation by more family members.

Essential to this entire process was that advice of the adolescent mother's parents was solicited and utilized in program planning. Parents have many personal needs such as advancing educationally, job training, etc. Parents got their message across: If you want us involved, you must survey our needs and develop programs that will not only meet our daughter's needs but out needs as well.

Program planners must be fully aware that involving the family may require long-term involvement with clients. The commitment for this time has to be made and adequately planned for, along with the allocation of appropriate staff. It requires a great effort to work with families who have many concrete and social needs. Also the coveted nine-to-five work day and the Monday through Friday work week may have to be altered to accommodate the schedules of working parents — both mothers and fathers.

This pilot project did not actively seek to involve the father of the adolescent mother's child. Some participated in the social activities because of their closeness with the adolescent mother's family. Services to adolescent mothers need to incorporate the baby's father where possible. However, if he does not have positive relationships with the adolescent mother and her family members, different intervention strategies may be required.

The Parent Aide Support Group Project was not a panacea for all problems nor successful in reaching all its goals. It is discussed here to exemplify many of the strategies vital to providing services from a familial context. Some of these strategies include: (1) home visits; (2) the use of local community workers; (3) meeting the concrete needs of the family; (4) program flexibility; (5) receiving feedback from parents about their personal needs; and (6) planning programs to address these needs. Specific planning should also include fathers — of the adolescent mother and of her child.

Some activities from this pilot program were incorporated into the Cities In School's regular programming. Vital components such as the use of community workers to solicit family participation, however, had to be terminated. The end of the Parent Aide Support Group is another example of the precarious funding of services for adolescent mothers.

SERVICES FOR FAMILIES: STRATEGIES

The extent to which a program with limited funding can broaden its focus to include families will vary, especially when an adolescent mother may be receiving services from several agencies simultaneously. When several agencies are involved with an adolescent mother, several questions come up: Should each agency involve the family? If yes, to what extent? Should there by one agency with the responsibility for coordinating the services to the family?

Answers to the very complex problems of providing services to adolescent mothers and their families are not all readily apparent. However, it is known that an adolescent's family is very much affected by the addition of an infant into the family. In turn, an adolescent mother and her child are very much affected by her family. We also know the family is deeply involved usually in parenting the new baby and generally provides more support to the adolescent mother than any other system. Regardless of what service the ado-

lescent mother uses, the family will have an impact on how that
service is utilized by the adolescent and thus the service has at least
an indirect — if not direct — impact on the family.

A hypothetical case illustrates this interdependence:

> An adolescent mother who returned to high school was using
> her siblings and friends as babysitters. She had to miss school
> frequently when a babysitter was not available. She had no
> money to pay for these services. After applying for and receiv-
> ing subsidized day care, it was found that the adolescent
> mother was not adhering to the eligibility requirements related
> to attendance, arrival and pick up times and the provision of
> personal belongings for the infant. She had been warned that
> the next infraction would result in termination from the day
> care program. The day care worker contacted the grandmother
> and informed her of the situation. The grandmother who
> worked was unaware that her daughter was abusing the day
> care services. The grandmother intervened and the adolescent
> began to abide by the policy of the day care center.

Although the adolescent mother was the primary beneficiary of
the day care services, it is evident family members were secondary
beneficiaries. They did not have to pay for the service and did not
have to rearrange schedules. They also no longer had to worry that
the child might be receiving inconsistent child care from babysitters
not always available.

Going back to the first question — should each agency involve the
family — our answer is an unequivocal yes. Family members are secondary recipients of services, and the family can also further enhance the use of services by an adolescent mother.

A framework for service delivery could rest on following continuum for levels of intervention: At a minimum, family members
should understand the nature of the services, eligibility requirements, how the services may impact on them, and how they can be
supportive to the adolescent mother and child. Counselors or indig-
enous workers who provide individual counseling about birth control, job training, nutrition, etc., should expand client systems to
provide family counseling. In-service training and ongoing consultation to staff should be provided where needed to enhance their
family counseling skills.

Along the continuum would be various levels of intervention.

Services might include referrals to meet concrete needs for any family member; one or two family sessions to resolve specific problems; counseling for the adolescent mother and father; and/or services aimed at one family member, such as a group for fathers of the adolescent mothers' children.

At the other end of the continuum, family therapy should be utilized to intervene with families who have more complex problems in functioning. Professionals should be utilized such as social workers, psychologists, nurses, or psychiatrists trained in family therapy. Problems may occur relating to new roles and additional responsibilities not only for the adolescent mother but for all family members. Decision making in relation to the child and who will discipline the adolescent mother and child may be needed. A decrease in leisure time, privacy, and finances for family members may come about. Family members should be helped to understand the very complex role conflicts for an adolescent mother who is being mothered while she herself is parenting (Authier & Authier, 1982).

Agencies must determine the extent to which they can involve families based upon the capacities and limitations of their agency. However, once the commitment is made by agency administrators to involve families, a change in focus can be made without major disruptions in service delivery.

Finally, one agency should have the responsibility for coordinating services to the family, thereby reducing fragmentation. Monitoring cases and referring individuals as well as the family unit for services to best meet their needs is at the heart of coordinating services. The concept of the case manager which has been used successfully to coordinate services for the mentally ill, might be quite effective with this population. This type of effort would very probably require funding from the federal government. Unfortunately, the present trend in federal spending is away from social programs. Therefore, the burden and the challenge rests with existing programs to incorporate the family of adolescent mothers into the structure of their service delivery system.

CONCLUSION

The literature documents the substantial assistance provided by family members in the care of the Black adolescent and her child. However, the literature does not give us an understanding of the psychological, social, and economic stresses placed on families. The Parent Aide Support Group Project drew attention to the social service and economic needs of families. Some families were in need of very concrete services. Others needed career counseling. It is also quite probable that some of these families had internal conflicts which could have used intervention by more skilled counselors. A myth perpetuated by many workers that needs dispelling is Black low-income families only want concrete services and are not interested in family counseling. Also many workers short-sightedly believe that the multiplicity of problems, many of which are related to economic status, guarantee that very little change can occur, they feel hopeless even to try. Research has shown, however, that may Black low-income families use family counseling appropriately and effectively (Goldstein, 1973; Lerner, 1972; Soloman, 1976). Therefore, workers where possible should provide outreach and concrete services, thereby building a trusting relationship that can foster deeper, possibly therapeutic intervention at the family level. Workers also need to assess clients differentially and assess the range of services needed by each family member. The essential point is that low-income clients should not be generalized and stereotyped but assessed on the basis of their strengths and needs.

Additionally, middle-class workers may not understand why many low-income Black adolescents have children and elect to keep them rather than have an abortion or give the infant up for adoption. Many workers lack knowledge of institutional racism and how it permeates every aspect of Black life. They lack understanding of the support provided through extended family and social relationships, and also lack the perspective to understand that until this nation shows Black youth they are part of its natural resources, Black youth will continue to prove their worth through demonstrated fecundity (Butts, 1983).[1]

With the many barriers to providing services from a family perspective, one wonders if the results will be worth the efforts involved. However, the approach does appear sound from a practical and theoretical viewpoint. Until it is tested, it is only speculation that, with enhanced family support, adolescent mothers may obtain and appropriately utilize services to help them advance educationally, obtain job training, and most importantly become better parents and well-adjusted adults. The results from the pilot project suggest that the barriers can be overcome and that benefits to the adolescent parents and their families are very much worth the energies and time expended.

NOTES

1. The Parent Aide Support Group was funded by the Region III Resource Center for Children, Youth and Families, Virginia Commonwealth University.
2. Cities In Schools Adolescent Health Center is a comprehensive, single-site project that provides medical, educational, and social services to teenagers and their families. Through a coordinated service delivery system, Cities In Schools is a leadership agency in a network linking teenage parents and their families to needed care and supplemental services in the District of Columbia.

REFERENCES

Authier, K. & Authier, J. (1982). Intervention with families of pregnant adolescents. In I. Stuart & C. Wells (Eds.), *Pregnancy in adolescence: Needs, problems, and management*. New York: Van Nostrand Reinhold Company.

Baldwin, W. (1982). Trends in adolescent contraception, pregnancy, and childbearing. In E. McAnarney (Ed.), *Premature adolescent pregnancy and parenthood*. New York: Grune and Stratton.

Baldwin, W. & Cain, V. (1980). The children of teenage parents. *Family Planning Perspectives, 12*(1), 34-43.

Bemis, J., Diers, E. & Sharpe, R. (1976). The teenage single mother. *Child Welfare, 50*(5), 309-318.

Biller, H. B. (1970). Mother absence and the personality development of the male child. *Developmental Psychology,* 181-201.

Billingsley, A. (1968). *Black families in White America*. New Jersey: Prentice-Hall, Inc.

Bolton, F. G. (1980). *The pregnant adolescent problems of premature parenthood*. Beverly Hills, California: Sage Publications.

Butts, J. D. (1981). Adolescent sexuality and teenage pregnancy from a Black perspective. In T. Ooms (Ed.), *Teenage Pregnancy in a family context: Implications for policy*. Philadelphia: Temple University Press.

Chilman, C. (1984). *Ecology of Adolescent Pregnancy and Parenting*. Keynote presentation. Howard University School of Human Ecology, Washington, DC.

Colletta, N. & Gregg, C. (1979, August). *The everyday lives of adolescent mothers: Variable related to emotional stress*. Paper presented at National Council on Family Relations Annual Meeting, Boston, MA.

Flaherty, E., Marecek, J., Olsen, K. & Wilcove, G. (1983). Preventing adolescent pregnancy: An interpersonal problem-solving approach. *Prevention in Human Services,* 49-64.

Forbush, J. & Maciocha, T. (1981). Adolescent parent programs and family involvement. In T. Ooms (Ed.), *Teenage pregnancy in a family context: Implications for policy*. Philadelphia: Temple University Press.

Furstenberg, F. (1981a). Implicating the family: Teenage parenthood and kinship involvement. In T. Ooms (Ed.), *Teenage pregnancy in a family context: Implications for policy*. Philadelphia: Temple University Press.

Furstenberg, F., Herceg-Baron, R. & Jemail, J. (1981b). Bringing in the family: Kinship support and contraceptive behavior. In T. Ooms (Ed.), *Teenage pregnancy in a family context: Implications for policy*. Philadelphia: Temple University Press.

Furstenberg, F. (1980). Burdens and benefits: The impact of early childbearing on the family. *Journal of Social Issues, 36*(1), 64-67.

Furstenberg, F. (1976), *Unplanned parenthood: The social consequences*. New York: The Free Press.

Goldstein, A. (1973). *Structural learning therapy: Toward a psychotherapy for the poor*. New York: Academic Press.

Harper, J. (1981). *Assessing the impact of social policies and programs on teenage mothers and their families*. Available from the Family Impact Seminar. Suite 310, 1001 Connecticut Avenue, N.W., Washington, DC 20036.

Hertz, H. D. (1977). Psychological implications of adolescent pregnancy: Patterns of family interaction in adolescent mothers-to-be. *Psychodynamics*, (18).

Hill, R. (1972). *Strengths of Black families*. New York: Emerson-Hall.

Jeffers, C. (1967). *Living poor*. Ann Arbor, MI: Ann Arbor Publishers.

Jones, B. A. (1983). The economic status of Black women. In J. D. Williams (Ed.), *The state of Black America (1983)*. New York: National Urban League.

Klerman, L. (1979). Design problems in evaluating service programs for school-age parents. *Evaluation and the Health Professionals*, (2)55-70.

Lerner, B. (1972). *Therapy in the ghetto*. Baltimore: The Johns Hopkins University Press.

McAdoo, H. (1978). Factors related to stability in upwardly mobile Black families. *Journal of Marriage and Family, 40*(4), 761-778.

McGhee, J. (1983). The changing demographics in Black America. In J. D. Williams (Ed.), *The state of Black America 1983*. New York: National Urban League.

Miller, S. H. (1983). *Children as parents, final report on a study of childbearing and child rearing among 12 to 15 year-olds*. New York: Child Welfare League of America.

Moore, K. A. (1981). Government policies related to teenage family formation and functioning: An inventory. In T. Ooms (Ed.), *Teenage pregnancy in a family context*. Philadelphia: Temple University Press.

Moynihan, D. P. (1965). The Negro family: The case for national action. Washington, DC: U.S. Government Printing Office.

National Center for Health Statistics (1983). *Monthly vital statistics report, 32*(9) (DHHS Publication No. (PHS)-84-1120). Hyattsville, MD: Public Health Service.

National Institute of Health (1982). *Adolescent pregnancy and childbearing – roles, trends and research findings from the CPR*. NICHD, Washington, DC.

Ooms, T. (1984). The family context of adolescent parenting. In M. Sugar (Ed.), *Adolescent parenthood*. New York: Spectrum Publications.

Placek, P. & Hendershot, G. (1974). Public welfare and family planning. *Social Problems, 21*, 658-673.

Presser, H. E. (1980). Sally's corner: Coping with unmarried motherhood. *Journal of Social Issues, 36*(1), 107-129.

Scales, P. (1981). Sex education and the prevention of teenage pregnancy: An overview of policies and programs in the United States. In T. Ooms (Ed.), *Teenage pregnancy in a family context: Implications for policy*. Philadelphia: Temple University Press.

Smith, E. W. (1975). The role of the grandmother in adolescent pregnancy and parenthood. *Journal of School Health, XLV*(5), 278-283.

Solomon, B. (1976). *Black empowerment: Social work in oppressed communities*. New York: Columbia University Press.

Sorenson, R. C. (1973). *Adolescent sexuality in contemporary America*. New York: World Publishing.

Stack, C. (1974). *All our kin: Strategies for survival in a Black community*. New York: Harper and Row.

Teenage Sexuality and Pregnancy (1982). Planned Parenthood of Metropolitan Washington, DC.

Zelnik, M. & Kantner, J. F. (1980). Sexual and contraceptive experience of young unmarried women in the United States, 1976 and 1971. In C. Chilman (Ed.), *Adolescent pregnancy and childbearing: Findings from research*. Washington, DC: U.S. Department of Health and Human Services (NIH Publication No. 81-2077).

Zelnik, M. & Kantner J. F. (1978). Contraceptive patterns and premarital pregnancy among women aged 15-19 in 1976. *Family Planning Perspectives*, (10), 135-142.

Reaching Black Male Adolescent Parents Through Nontraditional Techniques

Leo E. Hendricks
Annette M. Solomon

ABSTRACT. Despite considerable attention in the literature given to Black adolescent fathers by human service professionals (Hendricks, 1979, 1981, 1982, 1983), efforts to document how workers might reach out to them more have been few (Hendricks, 1983). Even less is available on how to reach Black adolescent fathers through nontraditional techniques, for new approaches are needed. As a step toward alleviating this nagging gap in the literature, this chapter utilizes data from studies conducted in Tulsa, Chicago, Columbus, Ohio, and Washington, DC to provide suggestions for reaching out to Black male adolescent parents through nontraditional means. Major issues include but are not limited to the following: (1) needs of Black male adolescent parents; (2) nontraditional techniques for reaching this group of parents; (3) planning the initial assessment meeting, including possible barriers to the process and

Leo E. Hendricks, MSW, MRP, PhD, is Associate Professor in the Urban Studies Program and in the Department of Community Health and Family Practice, College of Medicine, Howard University. He is also Director of Research at the Institute for Urban Affairs and Research at Howard. An epidemiologist, Dr. Hendricks serves as consultant to numerous state and federal agencies. He has published extensively on Black adolescent fathers and is a recognized scholar and teacher in this area. Annette M. Solomon, MSW, ACSW, is Director of Social Services for the Cities-In-Schools Adolescent Health Center in Washington, DC. This comprehensive center provides medical, educational, and social services to pregnant and parenting adolescents and their extended families. Ms. Solomon also does volunteer work with adolescents, conducting workshops on self-esteem, teenage pregnancy, reproductive health, etc. She has focused on the area of adolescent pregnancy for over eight years. The authors are grateful for research assistance and conducting interviews to Tony Hawkins, Michael McCoy, Teresa Montgomery, Janice Williams, and David Hooper; to Cleopatra S. Howard for supervising the field operations; to Dorothy J. Vance for typing the manuscript; and to Dr. Lawrence E. Gary, Director of the Institute for Urban Affairs and Research, for his support of this research. This article was made possible in part through award 1RO1-MH25551-01 from the Center for Minority Group Mental Health Programs (NIMH), and award 90CW637-01 from the Children's Bureau of Administration for Children, Youth and Families.

111

factors that contribute to its success; (4) do's and don'ts for helping Black adolescent fathers stay in treatment or in a counseling relationship; and (5) ways young Black fathers may be helpful not only to themselves but also the mothers and their children.

Some researchers have given persistent attention to the study of Black teen males as fathers (Hendricks, 1979, 1981, 1982, 1983). Efforts, however, to document how human service workers might reach out to them have been few (Kahn, 1982; Hendricks, 1983), while much less information is available on how to reach Black adolescent fathers through the use of newer nontraditional techniques. It is a small wonder then that human service workers express feeling quite uncomfortable about their endeavor to obtain knowledge on how they may reach out effectively to young Black male parents. Too many questions remain unanswered: What are the needs of Black male adolescent parents? What strategies and approaches are successful in reaching out to young Black fathers versus those that are not? In what ways may a young Black father be helpful not only to himself but also to the mother and his child?

As a step toward trying to put an end to this irksome gap in the literature, this chapter uses data from studies carried out in Tulsa, Oklahoma, Chicago, Illinois, Columbus, Ohio, and Washington, DC, as well as interviews with selected practitioners working with teen parents.

This research presumes that unmarried Black adolescent fatherhood is a stressful situation. For purposes of the study, stress was conceived as characterizing a discrepancy between demands impinging on a person—whether these demands be external or internal, challenges or goals—and the individual's (potential) responses to these demands (Mechanic, 1968). In shore, any or all forces to which a human being is subject may contribute to stress. Pertinent factors for discerning stress in unmarried teen fathers relate to the nature and outcome of each father's struggle with similar problems, notably the dilemmas of adolescence; his relationship with the unmarried mother; family, social, and economic pressures (Caughlan, 1960).

METHODS

The data are drawn from a cross-sectional study of 133 recent, first-time, unmarried Black adolescent fathers residing in Tulsa,

Oklahoma (N = 20); Chicago, Illinois (N = 27); Columbus, Ohio (N = 48); and Washington, DC (N = 38). Prior to the selection of the study population, an unmarried adolescent father was defined as an unwed male who was a father, or an acknowledged father-to-be, and under the age of 21 years. In addition to these criteria, subjects were required to be residents of either Tulsa, Chicago, Columbus, or Washington, DC.

Respondents were chosen with the help of social service staff from selected teen parenting agencies located in the cities identified above. By and large, these agencies offered educational, health, and social services to young women and their families. Also investigators were assisted in the identification and selection of the young fathers by the unwed teen mothers registered with these agencies when the studies took place.

All subjects, with the exception of the Washington, DC sample, were paid for their participation in this investigation. Subjects in Chicago were paid $5.00, those in both Columbus and Tulsa, $10.00.

Data were collected by four adult males and two adult females in face-to-face, private interviews. Questions pertained to the social and demographic traits of the population; their sexual knowledge, attitudes, and practices; problems they faced and how they coped; their relationships with the mothers of their children; and their interest in their children. Each subject was informed all information would be kept confidential and anonymous, and the he could refuse to answer a question or discontinue the interview at any time.

RESULTS

Table 1 provides some insight about who these young fathers are, according to the major socio-demographic variables chosen for this study. When comparisons were made among the four samples of fathers, important differences were found to exist among them. Young fathers in Tulsa and in Washington were more likely to be older at the birth or conception of their children than fathers in Chicago and Columbus (p < .01). Further, young fathers in Tulsa were more likely to have completed 12 or more years of school than were fathers in Chicago, Columbus, or Washington, DC (p < .01). In both Tulsa and Columbus, young fathers were more likely to be employed than those in Chicago and Washington (p = .05). In

Table 1

Distribution of Socio-Demographic Traits of Unmarried Adolescent Fathers by City

Traits	Tulsa N	Tulsa %	Chicago N	Chicago %	Columbus N	Columbus %	Washington D.C. N[a]	Washington D.C. %	p-value[b]
Age at birth or conception of child									
≤ 17	7	35	17	63	38	79	11	30	.01
≥ 18	13	65	10	37	10	21	26	70	
Age of first coital experience									
≤ 12	7	35	13	48	27	56	23	61	NS[c]
13-14	6	30	6	22	14	29	11	29	
15-17	7	35	8	30	7	15	4	10	
Family size									
≤ 3	4	20	4	15	9	19	5	13	NS
4	4	20	7	26	5	10	9	24	
≥ 5	12	60	16	59	34	71	24	63	
Father at home									
Present	13	65	15	56	29	60	13	34	.05
Not present	7	35	12	44	19	40	25	66	
Sisters who are unwed mothers									
Yes	8	40	12	44	25	52	20	53	NS
No	12	60	15	66	23	48	18	47	
Brothers who are unwed fathers									
Yes	7	35	8	30	17	35	18	47	NS
No	13	65	19	70	31	65	20	53	
Grade completed									
≤ 12	5	25	14	52	31	65	29	76	.01
≥ 12	15	75	13	48	17	35	9	24	
Employment status									
Employed	12	60	7	26	27	56	18	47	.05
Not employed	8	40	20	74	21	44	20	53	
Active church member									
Yes	8	40	11	41	11	23	6	16	.08
No	12	60	16	59	37	77	31	84	

[a]Missing value not included.   [b]p-value calculated by Chi-square statistics.
[c]Not statistically significant.

Washington, DC, subjects were more likely not active church goers (p = .08) and to have grown up in a house with one parent (p = .05). More generally, the fathers were likely to have had their first coital experience with a girl when they were 12 years old or less. Further, these young men usually came from families with at least five children. In fact, 65 percent of all fathers sampled were members of families with five or more children. No statistically significant differences were found among the fathers in regard to having siblings who were unwed parents; it was interesting to note that, with the exception of those in Washington, DC, these adolescent fathers were more likely to have sisters than brothers who were unwed parents.

Needs of Black Adolescent Fathers

The primary, essential characteristic of effective outreach to Black adolescent father is knowledge and understanding of their needs. Toward that end, fathers in this study were asked the question: "In your opinion, and from what you have seen yourself, what are some of the problems you have faced as a young father?" When taken together, problems encountered by these Black fathers suggest they need counseling about relationships as well as assistance with employment, job training, and education. For example, 46 percent indicated they had problems in a relationship or the problem was in the "other person." The nature of emotional and/or social difficulties for a father could be with his family of origin; restriction of his freedom imposed by responsibility for the child; the duty of providing for the child, or not being able to see his child as often as he would desire; problems with his girlfriend or unwed mother; problems with various members of the unwed mother's family; and not wanting the young woman to have the baby.

With regard to more external factors in the young men's lives, 34 percent of the fathers indicated problems related either to unemployment, lack of money, or not being able to finish school. Few of the Black fathers perceived their difficulties as the result of some personal failing. Those that did, indicated they were having a problem coping with being a father and setting a "good example" in the child's presence.

To obtain a clearer picture of what kinds of problems young Black fathers were likely to seek help with, they were asked: "When you ask someone for help with a personal problem, what types of problems do you discuss with them?" Chicago and Tulsa fathers were likely to bring up issues about themselves or about other external causes, especially employment. In contrast, a father in Columbus discussed with others problems that concerned another person more than discussing himself; while the Washington, DC

fathers probably discussed problems relating to relationships, financial responsibilities, or life goals.

"Who would you go to first with a problem?" Answers revealed
a majority of the young fathers — regardless of city of residence —
most likely went to their family first for help with a problem (Table
2). Subjects were next asked: "If you had a personal problem, who
or where would you go to for advice or help?" Responses indicated
a majority of the young fathers in each city would go to their mother
or father for advice or help, mostly to their mothers. This finding
was not too surprising since it was also found that when these young
Black fathers were growing up, a majority of them, in each city,
reported they were closer to their mothers than to other persons in
their family.

Clergy, friends, and school teachers were used rarely as a source
of help. Only one father from the entire study population said that
he would go to a minister. This was also not unexpected, as in each
of the four cities, a majority of the fathers were not active church
members. Only two of the fathers from the combined study population said they would seek help from a social service agency; however, data obtained from the Washington, DC sample revealed that
while young Black fathers were not prone to seek a social service

Table 2

Distribution of Responses by City to Question: "Who Would You Go To First
With a Problem?"

Source of Help With Problem

City	Family		Friend		Social Service Agency		Total	
	N	%	N	%	N	%	N	%
Tulsa	19	95	1	5	-0-	-0-	20	15
Chicago	23	85	4	15	-0-	-0-	27	21
Columbus	42	88	5	10	1	2	48	36
Washington, D.C.	31	84	5	13	1	3	37	28
Total	115	87	15	11	2	2	132	100

agency for help, 51 percent indicated they would seek out a human service agency if they wanted to know about their rights as a father and the rights of their children.

Feelings for the Mother and the Child

Human service workers must understand how a young father feels about the young mother and his child (Furstenberg, 1976; Pannor, 1970). When asked to describe the relationship between themselves and the young mothers both before and after the pregnancy, fathers were more likely to report that it was one of love, and 94-100 percent expressed an interest in their children's future.

OUTREACH TO YOUNG BLACK FATHERS: SUGGESTED STRATEGIES

In light of findings reported here, reaching out to Black adolescent fathers may be a difficult task because of the variation in their spiritual, physical, and concrete needs. Nevertheless, one may succeed in reaching out to the young Black male parent by employing a combination of traditional and nontraditional techniques. Workers need to accept the young Black father as he is and start out building a relationship with him in small ways. One way is to offer practical help, such as providing information to young Black fathers concerning their legal rights and responsibilities. This may include information about paternity suits, the legal significance of having the child bear his name if he does not marry the mother, the possible effect of fatherhood on his status as a student, and so on. In relation to schooling, practical assistance could be helping with arrangements for tutoring to return to school or to achieve a high school equivalency diploma (GED). Because a number of the fathers were observed to be unemployed, vocational counseling, training, and placement could help attract them to an established agency. Unless a human service worker can help resolve the young father's practical problems, it is difficult to focus on other less visible but important problems (Howard, 1975).

Meeting practical needs of young fathers, however, requires a special approach by an agency. Given that these fathers tended to receive sex education first from a friend, and tended to spend two to four days a week with their peers after school, work, or in the evenings, the use of peer counselors may be advisable. Through contacts at pool halls, basketball courts, and recreational centers, these counselors could be helpful to other human service workers in opening up communication with young fathers. Information concerning fathers' rights, sex education, the role of a father, and consumer education could be discussed freely. Some investigators (Howard, 1975; Johnson & Staples, 1979) caution, however, that these counselors must not act as "just a pal." If these counselors meet the young fathers in their own environment, the fathers want to feel the counselors have something special to offer.

In meeting the practical needs of young Black fathers, human service workers can also be aided by the young men's mothers, whom the majority of the respondents said they were closer to when growing up. Gottlieb (1975) has pointed out that mothers combined expert knowledge along with being the person who makes the greatest investment in the young man's well-being. Involving mothers or both parents of young fathers may make reaching young fathers easier.

This investigation, as noted, indicated that a majority of the fathers perceived their relationship with the mothers of their children to be one of love; they also expressed a marked interest in their children's future. If outreach efforts are predicated on the interest young fathers have for the mothers and their children, human service agencies will appear more accepting, and perhaps access will increase for all adolescents, including young fathers. Regardless of their motivation, young fathers are more likely to become involved if they are not threatened by an agency's sponsorship, its setting, or fear of legal action. Furthermore, once young fathers are involved in an agency program, it is critical to serve them after the birth of their child as well as before (Howard, 1975).

TREATMENT WITH ADOLESCENT BLACK FATHERS

While the knowledge base is far from complete or harmonious, some strategies and techniques have proved effective in outreach efforts to and in establishing positive relationships with Black adolescent fathers.

Adolescent mothers may bring a young father into a worker's office for a meeting. However, a joint counseling session is not recommended for the teen father's first visit. The relationship of the young woman and man may not be stable enough for such a meeting to be productive. Telephoning young fathers and offering to help with a personal problem especially around employment, job training, or employment counseling might constitute successful outreach. In fact, many workers find that meeting the employment needs of a teen father is a major step to unlocking the key to having a first meeting with him. Unless there is some tangible incentive for him, it is difficult to get the young father to come in for a counseling session.

Some practitioners have utilized the media (i.e., radio, television, and newspapers) to reach out to adolescent fathers. For example, one enterprising clinician reported attracting young males to a family planning clinic by placing advertisements in the Monday sports section of the local newspaper during the football season. Through these advertisements, young males were offered the following services that could be perceived as tangible rewards:

— physical examinations;
— diagnosis and treatment of sexually-transmitted diseases;
— sex education; and
— counseling.

The young men were told they could receive these services free of charge and on a walk-in basis. The results of these advertisements revealed that the younger teen males (17 and under) were likely to come into the clinic for physical examinations; older adolescent males (18 years or older) sought services for sexually-transmitted diseases.

Other workers report some success in reaching young fathers through public service announcements over radio and television. Others place posters with a message aimed at helping young fathers with their needs in pool halls, video arcades, around basketball courts, or wherever teen males are known to frequent. Another approach is to direct messages to mothers through posters placed in grocery stores.

Among the negatives is setting a specified time for the young father to come in for an interview. It is better to ask the young man something like the following to encourage him to come into the office: "Can you come in the morning, between the hours of thus and so? Or is the afternoon better for you, between the hours of thus and so?" To the extent it is possible, arrange the time for meeting with the young Black father at a time convenient for him. Also perhaps the meeting can be held at his home or some other mutually-agreed upon site.

Further the initial interview with a young Black father is crucial to a productive client-worker relationship. Failure to understand the young father's life circumstances may precipitate a mishandling of the first interview and prevent the possibility of even addressing the young father's presenting problem. A worker needs to be abreast of the state of Black America in general, and the local community, in particular. Does the young Black father come from a family living below the poverty level? From an intact or female-headed household? Are these clients sometimes school dropouts? Unemployed? Has the young father grown up in a neighborhood where most of the recreational facilities were so stressed and overcrowded they became a source of frustration and discontent? Answers to questions on this order may be obtained from several sources, including nonprofit organizations such as the Children's Defense Fund (1984) and the National Urban League (1984). Or information may be sought from local, state, or federal agencies dealing in these statistics.

The First Interview

Often, the life circumstances that help prompt the occurrence of a young Black father-worker interview manifest themselves in nonverbal communication during the interview. For example, nods, fingernail picking, slouched posture, lack of eye contact, and wearing either a hat, coat or jacket must not be overlooked, nor misinterpreted as hostile, uncooperative, or being closed or inarticulate. Not infrequently, practitioners report seeing a human service worker for any reason prompts a young Black male to make the statement: "I'm not crazy."

In addition to being abreast of the young father's life circumstances, it is important to be aware of complaints a young Black male parent may have toward human service workers. To that end, we learned in an interview with four Black adolescent males that these complaints may be of the following nature:

. . . Don't like the fact the conversations are taped. . . . Nobody likes to be on tape. . . .

. . . They (i.e., human service workers) tells you he doesn't think your problem is unique. You want to think it is or else you wouldn't go to see them. . . .

. . . They ask you a lot of questions that don't even pertain to the problem. Or are they just being nosy. . . .

. . . They "dig" into your past, your fears. People don't want to remember the past. . . . Rather leave those things in the past . . . leave the office worse off than when you came in. . . .

Further comments were made by these young Black males about what they disliked about their human service workers and their offices:

. . . Can't keep my hat on. It's (the hat) like a security blanket. . . .

. . . They (i.e., human service workers) don't seem to make . . . you feel comfortable. . . .

. . . They use big words I don't understand. . . .

. . . They sometimes try to use teenage slang and they sound stupid. . . .

. . . They are always writing while I talk. . . .

. . . They (i.e., the offices of human service workers) should have something that appeals to everyone — magazines, music. . . . Everyone doesn't drink coffee. . . .

. . . The offices are too clean. . . . They should look lived in. . . .

Young Black male parents tend to have several needs they define themselves as their priorities. Very often their priorities include the following:

— employment
— job skills training
— emergency financial assistance
— housing
— GED preparation, entry back into public schools, or entry into an alternative educational setting

Other needs may be less clearly stated and will need more defini-
tion. Wisdom dictates that a worker not attempt to assess all of a
young father's needs in the initial interview, especially since this
may engender misunderstanding or hostility between him and the
worker. It is far better to have a second visit with the young father to
complete the intake process. The initial assessment should focus on
the young father not on the worker's successful completion of required agency forms.

Moreover, it is not advisable or considerate during the young
Black father's initial visit to ask him a lot of questions or to discuss
goals, child support, and what he plans to do about the baby. Young
fathers often associate coming to a worker's office as reflective of
their being in some sort of trouble. Instead of talking a lot, listen
generously to the young father and let the interview center around
him, so he may express his concerns about the pregnancy if he
wishes. Put in another way, a worker might ask how becoming an
adolescent father has affected his life and what may be done to help
him with his immediate needs. Only after pressing concrete needs
are met does an adolescent father tend to entertain much discussion
concerning the young mother and his child. When these observations are taken in concert, they suggest strongly that the pregnancy
may be secondary to the young father's concrete needs.

Creating a comfortable therapeutic environment initially will encourage young Black fathers to return; more challenging material
should be saved for later sessions. Nonthreatening questions are
more appropriate for a Black adolescent father in the intake interview: his name, address, social security number, the name of a
person who may be contacted when the client can't be reached directly. What has his work experience been? Do not suggest con-
tacting or probing too deeply about his employer because his experience with his employer may be unfavorable. Trust, rapport, and
productive communication are likely to be established more readily
during an initial interview with the adolescent father, when he and
the worker sit side by side rather than being seated opposite one
another. This seating arrangement tends to promote honesty and
trust between the young father and the worker.

The Course of Treatment

Other factors may contribute to encouraging an adolescent father
to consider remaining in treatment:

1. During sessions, telephone conversations, and so on, address the young father as "Mr." until you gain his permission to call him by his first name.
2. Relax the young father by offering him a soft drink prior to the start of the session.
3. Have all calls held during sessions to contribute to his awareness that the counseling process and the young father's participation are important.
4. Have magazines displayed the young father may identify with, especially those having to do with sports.
5. Be apprised of the language the adolescent father may use since he may not have a good command of standard English.
6. Be prepared to discuss current events in the local community.
7. Keep interview session brief, no more than 45 minutes at a time.

Once a helping relationship with a young Black father stabilizes and concomitantly, some of his immediate needs have been addressed, the following areas are suggested for a Black teen father to work on, and it is hoped, achieve if they have bearing on that young father's life:

1. Standing by the unmarried mother, which lends some dignity to their relationship and is of extreme importance to her;
2. Participating in planning for the birth of their child;
3. Meeting financial responsibilities, if possible;
4. Examining thoughts and feelings revealed by the out-of wedlock pregnancy;
5. Recognizing the meaning and responsibilities of marriage and parenthood, if appropriate;
6. Developing a positive attitude toward getting help from the agency;
7. Understanding his attitudes and feelings toward the mother of his child;
8. Understanding this attitudes toward sex and the meaning and consequences of sexual relations; and
9. Recognizing his attitude toward fatherhood, which may include his seeing the child, and participating in parenting.

These areas, as well as an agency's role in providing assistance through its services, are proposed to the young Black father in the first few sessions with him and taken up again at appropriate times during ongoing counseling sessions (Rowan & Pannor, 1964; Pannor, 1963).

REFERENCES

Caughlan, J. (1960). Psychic hazards of unwed paternity. *Social Work, 5,* 29-35.
Children's Defense Fund (1984). *American children in poverty.* Washington, DC.
Furstenberg, F. F., Jr. (1976). The social consequences of teenage parenthood. *Family Planning Perspectives, 8,* 148-164.
Gottlieb, B. H. (1975). The contribution of natural support systems to primary prevention among four social subgroups of adolescent males. *Adolescence, 10,* 207-220.
Hendricks, L. E. (1983, December). *Unmarried adolescent fathers and their controls: The Washington, DC sample* (final report). Washington, DC: Howard University, Institute for Urban Affairs and Research.
Hendricks, L. E. (1983). Suggestions for reaching unmarried Black adolescent fathers. *Child Welfare, LXII,* 141-146.
Hendricks, L. E. (1982, August). *A comparative analysis of three select populations of Black unmarried adolescent fathers* (Final Report, Vol. 2). Washington, DC: Howard University, Institute for Urban Affairs and Research.
Hendricks, L. E. (1981, April). *An analysis of two select populations of Black unmarried adolescent fathers* (Final Report, Vol. 1). Washington, DC: Howard University, Institute for Urban Affairs and Research.
Hendricks, L. E. (1979, September). *Unmarried adolescent fathers: Problems they face and the ways they cope with them, the Tulsa, Oklahoma sample* (Final Report). Washington, DC: Howard University, Institute for Urban Affairs and Research.
Howard, M. (1975, Spring). Improving services for young fathers. *Sharing,* 10-22.
Johnson, L. B. & Staples, R. F. (1979). Family planning and the young minority male: A pilot study. *The Family Coordinator, 28,* 535-543.
Kahn, J. (1982, September-1983, January). *Fathers outreach report: Objectives and interventions.* Salt Lake City: University of Utah Medical Center.
Mechanic, D. (1968). *Medical sociology: A selective view.* New York: The Press.
National Urban League (1984). *The state of Black America, 1984.* New York: Communications Department, National Urban League, Inc.
Pannor, R. (1970). The forgotten man. *Nursing Outlook, 18,* 36-37.
Pannor, R. (1963). Casework services for unmarried parents. *Children, 10,* 65.
Rowan, M. & Pannor, R. (1964). *Casework with the unmarried father.* New York: Child Welfare League of America.

Adolescent Sexuality: Cultural and Legal Implications

Stanley F. Battle
Judith Lynn Rozie Battle

ABSTRACT. This chapter examines recent Supreme Court cases about issues of privacy rights pertaining to adolescent mothers, and also examines various presumptions the Court makes regarding adolescents. These case decisions are viewed in conjunction with a review of perspectives on Black adolescent parents. Overall, we contend that the Court's decisions do not take into consideration cultural differences within our society. Adolescents bear the brunt of this cultural dissonance and cannot look to the courts for understanding or increasing access. Sexuality, possible pregnancy, and childrearing for adolescents require legal provision for the rights of teens so they and their families can make appropriate decisions that respect privacy and cultural identity.

Historically, this nation has functioned on the premise that parents control and have authority for all decisions concerning their minor children. The courts and society embody this premise which is based on a presumption that parents always act in the best interest of their minor children. Unfortunately, there have been too many circumstances where this has not been true; the presumption has become too generalized.

Teenage pregnancy and its often concomitant problems have been

Stanley F. Battle, MSW, MPH, PhD, is Associate Professor of Welfare Policy, School of Social Work, and Associate Professor of Public Health in the Social and Behavioral Sciences Division at Boston University. Dr. Battle is the coordinator of the dual Public Health/Social Work program. He serves as consultant to several local, state, and federal programs. His research focus is on mental health issues affecting minorities, with a special interest in Black adolescent males. Judith Lynn Rozie Battle, MSW, JD, is Director of Affirmative Action and Human Rights in the Executive Office of Human Services for the Commonwealth of Massachusetts. She is also an Adjunct Assistant Professor in the School of Social Work at Boston University, where she teaches family law and children's rights. Ms. Battle has worked extensively in the child welfare area and is interested in the impact of the legal system upon families.

a major concern in this country for over a decade. Numerous cases have come before the Court to challenge the rights of parents, of adolescent parents and of the state. More recently, the concern for the rights of unborn fetuses has been brought before the Court. The courts are expanding responsibilities of women to their unborn fetuses, consequently interfering with an individual women's rights. The Supreme Court has had difficulty determining the rights of one interest over the rights of another interest.

The Court has not been competent in determining individual needs, and is too impersonal to scrutinize effectively the complex issues that have come before it. Consequently, decisions from the Court have been confusing and misleading. There have been numerous interpretations for each decision handed down, but there are still too many unanswered questions.

The Court has not effectively addressed the anomaly created when a minor adolescent suddenly becomes a minor parent. Daily issues arise affecting adolescent parents, particularly when they are dependent minors residing in their parents' homes. These issues include whether or not an adolescent female has the right to make a decision to use contraceptives independently from her parents; to make a decision regarding abortion independently from her parents; and whether an adolescent mother is considered competent enough to make *any* personal decisions independently from her parents.

The Court has not effectively addressed any of these concerns, and as a result, many adolescent mothers are uninformed regarding the legal consequences of sexual activity and eventual pregnancy. The underlying issue for many adolescent mothers is whether or not minor parents have an absolute right of privacy in any area.

This chapter reviews major Court cases regarding adolescent parents, and their right to privacy in contraceptive use, abortion, and general decisional privacy rights. Of special concern here is how these issues confront Black adolescent parents. "When private family affairs become public issues, it makes Americans uneasy, add race, and it puts us even more on edge" (Hulbert, 1984). Adolescent sexuality, as well as the course of pregnancy and childrearing, often reflects cultural identity.

THE RIGHT TO PRIVACY

Only as recently as 1965, in *Griswold v. Connecticut* did the Court first recognize the decisional privacy right. Although there were cases prior to *Griswold* alluding to the issue, this was the first case in which the Court so clearly specified the existence of the right. In *Griswold*, the Court invalidated a state statute prohibiting the use of contraceptives by married couples, finding that the Constitution grants a right of privacy to married couples making childbirth decisions. The Court later extended this holding in *Eisenstadt v. Baird* (1972), to include single adults under the Equal Protection Clause. The Court stated that

> if the right of privacy means anything, it is the right of the individual, married or single, to be free from unwarranted governmental intrusion into matters so fundamentally affecting a person as to the decision whether to bear or beget a child. (*Eisenstadt*, 1972)

The dilemma created for a teenage mother from the previous cases is the fact that she is a minor and not legally an adult. Although as early as 1920, some courts held that minor parents had a right to custody of their children (*Coates v. Benton*, 1920), there have been few certainties as to other rights for minors. Today the Court argues that adults and children are to be accorded different levels of state protection, and for this reason, all rights granted to an adult are not automatically granted to children. If a minor marries, this dilemma is somewhat alleviated because in every state a married minor is automatically emancipated and therefore usually considered a legal adult (Sussman & Guggenheim, 1980).

In 1967, the Court decided *In Re Gault*, which found children entitled to the same constitutional rights and privileges afforded adults. *Gault* concerned a 15-year-old probationer found delinquent after being apprehended, following a verbal complaint that he made lewd or indecent remarks over the telephone to a neighbor. The Court stated that "neither the Fourteenth Amendment nor the Bill of Rights is for adults alone" (*Gault*, 1967). This decision indicates a child has the same constitutional protections as an adult, yet the Court has carved out numerous exceptions, based on concern for either parents rights, states rights, or both.

As previously noted, the Court functions of the presumption that parents always act in the best interest of their children; therefore, parents should have control over any minor dependent children, particularly those residing at more. Historically, this presumption rests on the attitude that children were the property of their parents.

Although children are not seen today as property, the Court views parental decisions about their children as intrafamilial concerns. The Court prefers not to interfere unless parents' interests are in conflict with state interests. However, in many instances, parents' interests and adolescent parents' interests are in conflict, particularly around the issues of contraception, abortion, adoption, and childrearing.

Although there are times when parents may best determine the interest of their child, they are still a third party making decisions for the child. Therefore, there are instances when there is a need for the state — acting as parens patriae — to intervene to neutralize the conflicting interests of the adolescent mother and her parents. Usually the state's purpose in intervening is because either the adolescent's or her parents' interests are against a significant state interest. Often the state's interest is more closely aligned with the parents' interests. For example, several court rulings have allowed parents' interests to prevail as long as states' interests were not diminished. In *Meyer v. Nebraska* (1923), the right of parents to have their children taught German in parochial school was protected against state interference. Parents' free exercise claims were upheld in *Pierce v. Society of Sisters* (1925); parents were accorded the right to educate their children in parochial schools. More recently in *Wisconsin v. Yoder* (1972), the Court upheld the right of Amish parents to remove their children from public schools and instead provide them with community-sponsored vocational training in keeping with their religious beliefs. The state interest in all of these cases was to educate children, and in each situation this interest was not ignored by parental interests. Instead the Court approved parental alternatives to reach the same end (Sher, 1983).

These cases established the limited right of parents to make certain educational, religious, and moral decisions for their children. It is this series of cases the Court cites when deciding that dependent adolescent mothers are under the control and authority of their parents. Despite the fact an adolescent mother may be mature and competent enough to make her own decisions, the court has continued to cite cases purporting parental rights to rear children as they desire. *Gault* gave minors important liberty interests independent of their parents; these gains have been subordinated.

Clearly there are two conflicting groups of cases: One holds that children have certain constitutional rights, the other that parents have the right to rear their children as they see fit. These two groups of cases appear unable to co-exist.

Further, a third series of cases appears to conflict with the previous two. These cases address various state interests. Although two interests may be the same or similar, usually the two interests are the state and parental. For example, in *Ginsberg v. New York* (1968), both the parents and the state had an interest in preventing the sale of pornographic magazines to minors.

THE RIGHT TO CONTRACEPTION AND ABORTION

In the area of contraceptive use, decisional privacy rights were first granted to adults in *Griswold* (1965). In 1977, the Court decided *Carey v. Population Services International*, recognizing minors' privacy rights: The Court invalidated a New York law prohibiting the sale of contraceptives to minors. The state had claimed an interest in deterring sexual activity among adolescents, but the Court disapproved of the means chosen. The Court felt that although state interest in deterring sexual activity among adolescents was legitimate, alternative methods were available to the state; the state had not shown that their means would in fact achieve the end sought.

In *Carey*, the Court utilized a rational test weighing the interests of adolescents against the state's interest, and determined that the privacy rights of the adolescent outweighed the interest of the state because of the means the state had chosen to achieve its end. It is clear the Court would have upheld the prohibition if the state had chosen a better method to achieve its stated goal. With this understanding it is apparent adolescent contraceptive decisions are subject to the particular state's ability to choose a method of prohibition that effectively surmounts rational tests utilized by the Court.

Another area of confusion for adolescent mothers is the right to an abortion. In *Roe v. Wade* (1973), the Court held that a right of personal privacy existed under the Constitution, and this right "is broad enough to encompass a women's decision whether or not to terminate her pregnancy" (*Roe*, 1973). *Roe* extended the privacy rights of *Griswold* to abortion during the first trimester. Again the Court's decision addressed adult women, so that a minor adolescent mother was left in a dilemma: Did she too have a right to make a privacy decision regarding abortion?

Eventually, in *Planned Parenthood of Central Missouri v. Danforth* (1976), the Court addressed the issue of adolescent mothers regarding abortion: The state has no constitutional authority to give a third party an absolute veto over the decisions of a doctor and patient to terminate a patient's pregnancy. The Court felt that when a minor was involved, there was an extra step which the Court would have to take. The Court would need to look to whether or not there was any significant state interest in conditioning an abortion for a minor, that would not be present in the case of an adult women. In other words, the Court held that a state may not require an absolute blanket parental consent for a minor's abortion. The Court stated, "Any independent interest a parent may have in the termination of the minor daughter's pregnancy is no more weighty than the right of privacy of the competent minor mature enough to have become pregnant" (*Danforth*, 1976).

This decision raises the question of how the Court determines who is a "competent minor." Certainly, the Court is not the appropriate entity to make this decision. There are many theories of what constitutes competency, ranging from single characteristics to combinations of such characteristics as age, maturity, intelligence and knowledge.

The second Court decision—*Bellotti v. Baird* (1979)—recognized the states' special interest in encouraging an unmarried pregnant minor to seek the advice of parents in deciding an abortion. The adolescent in *Bellotti* challenged the constitutionality of a state statute that required parental consent before a minor could obtain an abortion, and provided for judicial review of a parent's decision to deny permission. The Court found that the statute unconstitutionally restricted the abortion rights of minors. Although the Court did not find parents had an absolute right to prevent their daughters' abortions, the minor's access to an abortion is contingent upon having sufficient maturity and knowledge. The Court again differentiates between the privacy rights of adults and minors by relying on the presumptions of immaturity and diminished capacity.

In summary, the Court has not required absolute blanket parental consent for all adolescents attempting to obtain an abortion. Instead the Court has placed a burden on each individual to show she is an exception because she is mature and knowledgeable about the consequences of what she is doing. Yet placing the burden of proving a pregnant adolescent is an exception is not the usual method utilized by the Court. Traditionally, it has been the state's burden to demonstrate that an adolescent mother is not mature and knowledgeable about her decision.

Finally, in *H. L. v. Matheson* (1981), the Court upheld a Utah state statute requiring parental notification before an unmarried, un-emancipated minor could obtain an abortion. The Court stated that

> although minors are protected by such constitutional rights,
> the state statute that is rationally related to a significant state
> interest can overcome the qualified constitutional rights of mi-
> nors when the state interest in protecting minors is different
> from it interests in protecting adults. (*Matheson*, 1981)

The holding of this case is extremely narrow. It specifically speaks to unmarried adolescents living with and dependent on their parents. The Court places a tremendous burden on all adolescents seeking an abortion. They will now have to prove their interest would not be served by notification of parents; that family integrity would not be served by the notification; and that they are mature enough to make this decision on their own. This is an unfair, too weighty expectation to place on an adolescent. As noted, when a state statute restricts a constitutional right, traditionally the respon-sibility of the state has been to prove its significant interest is ration-ally related to its objective. The holding of this case diminishes the right of decisional privacy for most adolescent mothers.

Matheson also addresses the issue of notification of parents rather than consent from parents. This distinction is important be-cause the Court has not overruled previous decisions not requiring blanket parental consent. In this case the Court is seeking to have an adolescent mother communicate with her parents regarding impor-tant personal privacy decisions, not requiring her to obtain ap-proval.

However, the Court lays out three presumptions which further deteriorate the fundamental rights of adolescent mothers. The dicta of the case explains the Court's approach in reaching its decision:

1. Implicit in the Court's analysis is the presumption that preg-nant adolescents seeking abortion are immature.
2. Notice to parents would serve a state interest in preserving family integrity.
3. Finally, the Court implied that the states' interest in an adoles-cent's health was served by parental notification.

It is unfortunate the Court made these presumptions. The Court is not the appropriate entity to make such decisions and had no factual information to prove or disprove its presumptions. As previously stated, the danger with these presumptions is the tremendous burden placed on future adolescent mothers who wish to challenge a parental notification requirement.

Hence a review of the cases indicates a hesitancy on the part of the Court to grant equal constitutional rights to minors and adults — in spite of the fact that the Court in *Gault* stated that the Constitution is *not* for adults only. The Courts have been willing to go only so far in granting privacy rights in areas of contraception and abortion to adolescents, stubbornly holding onto the presumption that parents or the state (acting as parens patriae) know what is best for adolescent mothers. Because each adolescent mother is an individual, she should not be unfairly grouped nor presumed to have diminished abilities. Despite the fact that the Court allows an adolescent mother to prove she is an exception, there are definite limitations because of court costs and legal fees which most adolescent mothers could not afford. For poor Black teens the barriers are even higher.

Another important concern the Court apparently does not address is the fact that when an adolescent mother expresses a desire not to confide in her parents, there may be a very good reason for this reluctance. She has lived with her parents and generally has a better idea of how they will react to her dilemma. Therefore, the Court should not attempt to force family communication without really considering the family culture and structure.

THE BLACK FAMILY PERSPECTIVE

Too often professionals tend to perceive Black families in need as dysfunctional if the families deviate too far from the traditional Western, middle-class, male-dominated pattern, ideally consisting of an employed husband, wife at home and their biological children. Deviancy from this norm generated hypotheses concerning partial causality for a myriad of social problems (delinquency, truancy, etc.). However, today and within the last decade, the traditional American family structure has been changing due to the incidence of working wives (dual career households), live-in arrangements, gay and lesbian living arrangements, co-operatives, etc. Much of this newer approach to family life emerged during the American youth movement (post Civil Rights era) of the 1970s. The impact of White youth—and many of their elders—matriculating into such family patterns has been that what was viewed as "deviant" is currently "normal" (Taborn & Battle, 1984).

Despite the welter of social problems Blacks face, they continue to marry, establish families, and make positive contributions to society (Grier & Cobbs, 1972). Practitioners must be aware that the two vitally important cultural missions of the Black family are survival and providing an accurate interpretation of the world to their children. Culturally Blacks believe their children must learn how to survive in an indifferent, racist world. These same Black children will survive and provide the foundation for the future.

Concern about the effects of Court decisions on Black adolescent mothers springs from the frustration that teenage parenthood is disproportionately a Black problem. Black girls—of whom there are far fewer than White ones—have more than half the babies born to single teenagers—in 1980, roughly 134,000, compared to 131,000 White births (Hulbert, 1984).

Consequently, laws based on middle-class, White values mean poor, Black teenagers will be viewed as deviant and will come before the courts in disproportionate numbers on issues of contraception and abortion.

FAMILY PLANNING

Family planning programs in 1975 were located in 79 percent of the counties in the United States, and served 1.3 million adolescent patients. Approximately the same number of adolescents received contraceptive care from the private physicians. It is believed that 117,000 births to teenagers and 250,000 abortions were averted in 1979 through family planning clinic enrollment (Freeman, 1982). Between October 1977 and August 1978, Freeman collected data from two groups of urban Black adolescents on attitudes toward contraception. The 730 participants included 358 female high school students, 249 male students, and 123 females in teen clinics. The findings indicated that *both* Black male and Black female students felt that responsibility for contraception belonged to both sexes. However, Black males were *less likely* to recognize the risk of pregnancy, had less information about contraceptives, and expressed less support of contraceptive use than Black females in the same classes. In addition, males were likely to believe that females didn't have correct information about contraception, an attitude that decreased involvement. It is quite possible that contraceptive use is perceived by Black males as being for females only; thus responsibility may be an issue, as Hulbert comments (1984):

> During the 1970s sexual activity among Black teenage girls did not increase markedly, and soon leveled off—but at significantly higher levels than among White girls. Sixty-five percent of single Black teenagers in 1979 were sexually experienced, compared to 42 percent of Whites; and on average they start having sex a year earlier, at 15 and a half.

It is difficult to obtain a clear understanding of how many abortions Black adolescents have nationwide because the percentages usually combine Black with non-White groups, thereby presenting a distorted image. "Although abortions have risen among Black, as among White, teenagers, the totals are different: 34 percent of the pregnant Black girls have abortions, compared to 40 percent of White girls" (Hulbert, 1984).

Generally because of religious values, family (the extended family concept), and personal perceptions of abortions, Blacks are not generally in favor of abortions. In 1980, there were an estimated 44,942 *legal* abortions by Whites as compared with 8,106 abortions by Blacks. Discussion of abortion in the Black community is an emotional issue, and is not viewed as a means of birth control. In the final analysis, it is critical that beliefs and values be weighed by the female and male in order to make the best decision for their well-being (Taborn & Battle, 1984).

Two-thirds of births to all unmarried teenagers are unintended. Most unwed teenage mothers tend not to give up their babies for adoption. In the case of Black adolescents, it is quite common for their mother, grandparents, aunts and uncles to rear their children. Traditionally, only a very small number of Black adolescents formally give up their babies. In 1971, adoption or care by family members was more common: 87 percent of all teenage mothers (75% among Whites, 94% among Blacks) kept their children (Guttmacher, 1981).

Clearly Black adolescent mothers are keeping their children who receive a great deal of love and attention from the family. Black children project for family a sense of roots, firmness and future. They constitute a symbolic expression of womanhood for many Black adolescent mothers and permit the open expression of unconditional love. Demography is implicity (if not explicitly) understood in the Black community, causing Black mothers to view adoption as a last resort.

It is necessary that human service programs, as well as the Courts, when working with Black adolescent parents consider the influence which many of the aforementioned factors might have on the client's family system (Taborn & Battle, 1984).

CONCLUSION

The Court has not, as is also true with social service professionals, taken into account the racial, cultural or economic life of individuals who must abide by its decisions. Yet the court continues to make decisions based on Western societal values that are binding on everyone. There is an assumption that all families are supportive, loving, and financially secure enough to contend with the problems that can occur as a result of teenage pregnancy. Clearly there is an

> inherent unfairness in the unitary family law that is applied in the United States to many diverse cultural and ethnic groups. American family law is basically middle class. Perhaps a socially fair balance could be struck between majority law and minority cultures at the point where special regulation and allowance for cultural diversity begins to conflict with the rights of others. (Krause, 1977)

The Court's recent requirement of parental notification in abortion cases is an unprecedented interference into intrafamilial communications and relationships. This interference may have extremely serious consequences for teenage mothers. In many family situations the Court's interference may be too much or too little too late. In other words, for some adolescent mothers the requirement of parental involvement may force a young woman to seek unorthodox abortions. This may lead to physical as well as emotional difficulties for the teen mother, if not death. On the other hand, there are familial situations where the parents are just not the appropriate models for an adolescent to turn to, whether for reasons such as child abuse, previous sexual abuse, or an unsupportive family environment.

The Court's decisions really have created more confusion for families and particularly for adolescents.

With improved efforts to take cultural differences into consideration, social service programs can effectively work with adolescent mothers and their families without the Court's interference. These agencies employ professionals who are trained to work with individuals and families. The Court does not have these professional skills and is usually left to rely on an individual state's interpretations as to which interests are most important and significant. However, state interests are also based upon values which do not take into consideration all classes, races or cultures of people in our society.

REFERENCES

Bellotti v. Baird, 443 U.S. 622 (1979).

Bridge, B. (1982). Parent and child: *H. L. v. Matheson* and the new abortion litigation. *Wisconsin Law Review*, 17-116.

Buchanon, E. (1982). The Constitution and the anomaly of the pregnant teenager. *Arizona Law Review,* 24, 553-610.

Bush, S. (1982). Parental notification: A state-created obstacle to a minor woman's rights to privacy. *Golden Gate University Law Review,* 12, 579-603.

Byrne, T. (1982). Right to abortion limited: The Supreme Court upholds the constitutionality of parental notification statutes. *Loyola Law Review,* 28, 281-296.

Carey v. Population Services International, 431 U.S. 678 (1977).

Coates v. Benton, 80 Okla 93, 194 (1920).

Eisenstadt v. Baird, 405 U.S. 438 (1972).

Freeman, E. W. (1982, August). Never-pregnant adolescents and family planning programs, contraception, continuation, and pregnancy risk. *American Journal of Public Health.*

Ginsberg v. New York, 390 U.S. 629 (1968).

Goldstein, J., Freud, A. & Solnit, A. (1979). *Before the best interests of the child.* New York: The Free Press.

Grier, W. & Cobbs, P. (1972). *Black rage.* New York: Basic Books, Inc.

Griswold v. Connecticut, 381 U.S. 479 (1965).

Guttmacher Institute. (1981). *Adolescent pregnancy.* New York: Guttmacher Institute.

H. L. v. Matheson, 450 U.S. 398 (1981).

Hulbert, A. (1984, September 10). Children as parents. *The New Republic.*

In Re Gault, 387 U.S. 1 (1967).

Keiter, R. (1982). Privacy children and their parents: Reflections on and beyond the Supreme Court's approach. *Minnesota Law Review,* 66, 459-518.

Krause, H. (1977). *Family law.* St. Paul: West Publishing Co.

Meyer v. Nebraska, 262 U.S. 390 (1923).

Pierce v. Society of Sisters, 268 U.S. 510 (1925).

Planned Parenthood of Central Missouri v. Danforth, 438 U.S. 52 (1967).

Roe v. Wade, 410 U.S. 113 (1973).

Sher, E. (1983). Choosing for children: Adjudicating medical care disputes between parents and the state. *New York University Law Review,* 58, 157-205.

Sussman, A. & Guggenheim, M. (1980). *The rights of parents.* New York: Avon Books.

Taborn, J. & Battle, S. (1984). *Working with the Black adolescent parent.* Minneapolis: Control Data Corporation.

Wisconsin v. Yoder, 406 U.S. 205 (1972).

Index

for Black adolescent mothers, 99-107,
  108
  crisis orientation approach of, 100
  funding problems of, 100-101
  multiple use of, 100
  Parent Aide Support Group,
    101-105,109n.
for Black families, 97,101-108,109
improvement of, 56
increase of, 56
social development and, 56
Social skills, of Black adolescent
  mothers, 55
Socioeconomic factors, in sexual activity,
  28
Supreme Court decisions
  regarding abortion, 129-132,135
  regarding contraception, 126-127,
    129-130,132

T

Teachers
  influence on sexual activity, 77,78
  sexual permissiveness attitudes of, 80,
    82,83,84,85,86-87,88,90,91,92

W

Welfare assistance
  to Black adolescent mothers, 97-98
  Black adolescent mothers' perception
    of, 62,63,66,67,69
  to Black female-headed households,
    97-98
  to illegitimate children, 17
  out-of-wedlock pregnancy correlation,
    33
White adolescent females
  abortion rate among, 134
  age at menarch, 3
  birthrate, out-of-wedlock, 1,16,133
  sexual activity experimentation by, 4,
    134
White adolescent mothers
  children kept by, 134
  infant mortality rate among, 2
White adolescents, contraception use by,
  7-8
White females, as heads of households,
  17